LEEDS COLLEGE OF BUILDING LIBRARY
CLASS NO.
BARCODE

KT-244-952

*How to support and*
*teach children with*
# special educational
# needs

**Veronica Birkett**

LEEDS COLLEGE OF BUILDING
WITHDRAWN FROM STOCK

LDA

# Acknowledgements

The author would like to thank Jo Browning Wroe for her encouragement and support in the early days of writing. She would also like to acknowledge the work and dedication of the many teachers and teaching assistants she has observed, who have provided the inspiration for this book. Thanks also go to her daughters, Sally, Lucy and Hannah, for their pride, support and encouragement. And of course, last but not least, thanks must go to the excellent LDA team for providing invaluable support and also the expertise to transform the manuscript into an eminently readable and attractive book.

For extra copies of this book please call Customer Services on 0845 120 4776.

Every effort has been made to obtain permission for the inclusion in this book of quoted material. Apologies are offered to anyone to whom it has not been possible to contact.

Permission to photocopy
This book contains resource sheets which may be reproduced by photocopier or other means for use by the purchaser. This permission is granted on the understanding that these copies will be used within the educational establishment of the purchaser. This book and all its contents remain copyright. Copies may be made without reference to the publisher or the licensing scheme for the making of photocopies operated by the Publishers' Licensing Agency.

The right of Veronica Birkett to be identified as author of this work has been asserted by her in accordance with sections 77 and 78 of the Copyright, Designs and Patents Act 1988.

How to support and teach children with special educational needs
MT00605
ISBN-13: 978 1 85503 382 5
© Veronica Birkett
Cover illustration © Peter Wilks
Inside illustration © Rebecca Barnes
All rights reserved
First published 2003
Reprinted 2004 (May, July), 2005, 2006, 2007

Printed in the UK for LDA
Abbeygate House, East Road, Cambridge, CB1 1DB, UK

# Contents

Contents

# Foreword

The aim of this book is to provide clear guidelines for schools to support their efforts with teaching and supporting pupils with special educational needs (SEN) in primary and secondary schools.

## Who will benefit from this book?

Senior management teams – who may wish to review and assess their existing practice and arrangements in schools regarding the management, support and teaching provided for pupils with SEN.

SENCos – who may wish to consider their role and responsibility towards teachers, teaching assistants and pupils with SEN.

Teachers in primary and secondary schools – who are interested in enhancing their existing skills in order to support and teach pupils with SEN. The ideas offered for the management of teaching assistants are one aspect of this.

Teaching assistants – who will find the book is a useful indicator of the possibilities of their role and extends their knowledge of effective ways of supporting and teaching pupils with SEN.

Much of what goes on in schools to support pupils with special needs is underpinned by legislation and official documentation. See References, page 63 for information.

# Part 1
# The challenge

## The current state of play

The right of pupils with special needs to receive an education in mainstream schools has become a very significant issue in recent years. Many pupils with highly complex needs are now included in mainstream schools, and teachers must find ways to support them. The Special Educational Needs and Disability Act 2001 (known as SENDA) sets out requirements for schools which make it unlawful to discriminate without justification against disabled pupils and any other prospective pupils. Schools have a duty not to treat disabled pupils less favourably than others and a duty to make reasonable adjustments for them. For teachers, this presents a challenging task: raising standards of achievement for all pupils and at the same time including and providing for pupils with SEN. How can this be achieved?

Enter the teaching assistant (TA).

The idea of employing additional adults in the classroom to support teachers is comparatively new. The Plowden Report (Central Advisory Council for Education 1967) did identify a group of non-teaching staff in schools, but these were not commonly to be found there.

My own teaching career began in the swinging sixties. For years I had a class of over forty children without another adult in sight. This even included the times when I took my class to the swimming baths by using the public bus service. All that occupied my mind on the hazardous walk back was the hope that the first bus that turned up would accommodate all of us, so we wouldn't have to wait for hours for one that could.

As for pupils with SEN, I never encountered any, unless you included the pupils in 'C' streams, who were judged to be the least academic. Most pupils with disabilities were in 'special schools' and some were not in school at all. The 1944 Education Act gave all pupils, other than those with severe learning difficulties, the right to receive an education. The Handicapped Children's Act 1970 finally gave all children the right to an education.

Change, at last, was afoot. The government set up the Warnock Committee in 1974 to have a closer look at just what was going on regarding pupils with difficulties and disabilities. The Warnock Report was produced in 1978, and led directly to the Education Act 1981. The Act was to be of great significance for pupils with SEN. Cowne (1998) says, 'the 1981 Act influenced attitudes of teachers in mainstream schools. They began to recognise pupils with special educational needs were their responsibility. Integration policies were adopted by many LEAs and schools. Training . . . was funded through training grants from 1983 onwards (DES circulars 3/83–86).'

*'As teachers we want to do our very best for all our pupils. They are all special.'*

These moves had an impact on my own life as a teacher in the 1980s. My school, mindful of the 1981 Act, set up a withdrawal class for pupils with learning difficulties. The responsibility for this was given to me, and soon I had invited two volunteer mums, with minimum training (from me), into school daily to assist with the delivery of a 'remedial programme'. Thank you, Dot and Val. I couldn't have done without you!

That is how things were then, reliant on goodwill. The potential of the Dots and Vals was clear, however, and schools were beginning to employ more and more adults to give support officially within classrooms. These adults, often known as classroom ancillaries, tended to have more involvement with classroom organisation than the support of pupils' learning.

The TAs of today are closely involved with the teaching of pupils, as is reflected in their current title, although some schools refer to TAs working with pupils with SEN as learning support assistants. Whatever their title, they are now regarded as a valuable and indispensable part of the school team and the number of TAs employed in our schools has increased dramatically over recent years. There are several reasons for this:

- The introduction of the Code of Practice on the Identification and Assessment of Special Educational Needs in 1994. This required that schools should identify and make provision for all pupils with SEN and that some help and support should be provided. This was to be in addition to the support already provided by assistants employed to work with pupils with statements. Schools began to employ many more TAs to support identified pupils.

- Recent government policies which have promoted both social and emotional inclusion. Schools need to find ways of coping with dysfunctional behaviour. Many TAs have been employed to offer support to pupils.

- The recent government initiatives to raise standards in general, for example the introduction of the literacy and numeracy strategies in primary schools. These have been accompanied by the employment of TAs to support the teacher and increase their efficiency.

- The Special Educational Needs and Disability Act 2001 further increased the opportunities for pupils with disabilities to be educated in mainstream schools. More pupils with disabilities means more TAs are needed.

So, things have changed since the sixties. It is clear that the skills and knowledge required of senior management teams, teachers and TAs are very different from what they were.

Schools need to find ways to address the diverse and complex needs of the many pupils with SEN who are now included in mainstream schools, and also to take full account of the equally special needs of the rest of the class. As teachers we want to do our very best for all our pupils. They are all special.

Read on, this book will help you to achieve this aim.

# Responsibilities of senior management

The role of teachers and TAs in the support of pupils with SEN will be influenced by the efficiency of senior management. The introduction of TAs is crucial in meeting the needs of pupils requiring additional support, and clearly the quality and quantity of the assistants is important. That is the responsibility of the senior management team, and it will be affected by funding available.

Some teachers, while appreciating the valuable support offered by TAs, find the task of managing them somewhat daunting. Barbara Lee (2002), following extensive research, identified a number of factors for effective working with TAs. The efficiency of senior management in addressing the issues she lists will have a significant impact on how teachers, TAs and SENCos undertake their responsibilities towards pupils with SEN. Her list may be used by senior management teams:

○ *Clarity of role.* Teachers and TAs need to be aware of exactly what the latters' role entails. It should be clearly outlined in the job description, and teachers and TAs should be given copies. Schools usually produce two outlines: the role of TAs offering general support differs from that of those working with pupils with SEN.

○ *Induction and support.* Many schools provide TAs with a mentor – usually an experienced TA – to act as a support for the first week. During this time, the newly appointed TA may observe others working with pupils with SEN, both in the classroom in a group situation and offering support to individual pupils with statements. The following factors will also help the induction procedure. TAs should be:

　○ given recommendations of relevant reading material;
　○ shown the resources for pupils with SEN;
　○ advised about the purpose of IEPs;
　○ provided with a ring binder if they are to work with specific pupils (see page 17);
　○ shown the record-keeping system and given the opportunity to practise completing review meeting report sheets (see page 11) and record sheets (see page 17).

○ *Consideration of deployment of TAs.* Many heads, given adequate funding, would like to provide a full-time TA in every class, but juggling the budget usually means compromise. Preference for the placement of the TA will usually be given to:

　○ difficult or large classes;
　○ classes with large numbers of SEN pupils;
　○ inexperienced teachers;
　○ classes shared by two teachers (the TA's presence offers some consistency to pupils with SEN).

○ *Job description.* All TAs should be provided with a job description which, in the case of those employed to work with pupils with SEN, may resemble the one on page 8:

### Job description

**TAs employed to work with pupils with statements or in need of additional support**

#### Main responsibilities

○ To support named children protected by a statement of SEN or who are in need of additional support owing to learning or other difficulties.

○ To work under the guidance of the SENCo, head teacher and appropriate class teachers.

#### Special conditions

○ The TA will be made aware of the relevant contents of the statement of SEN, if the pupil has one.

○ The TA will be made familiar with the pupil's individual education plan (IEP).

#### Main functions

○ To minister to the physical needs of the child with reference to guidance on first aid in schools and the school policy on the administration of medicines.

○ To support the child in all areas of the curriculum, as directed by the class teacher.

○ To support the child as a member of a collaborative group.

○ To help the child develop both social and organisational skills.

○ To monitor the child's work and keep appropriate records.

○ To carry out specific programmes of work devised to meet the child's needs.

○ To assist in the planning of relevant activities.

○ To prepare appropriate materials.

○ To liaise with parents and professionals.

○ To work within the general aims of the school and to contribute to its overall ethos.

○ To undertake related activities as directed by the head and the SENCo.

○ *Clear line management.* Teachers and TAs need to be aware of who their line manager is. For those working with pupils with statements and School Action Plus pupils, the SENCo should be the main line manager. TAs working with pupils at School Action are often managed by the class teacher.

● *Time for teachers and TAs to collaborate*. Often pre-school meetings need to be arranged, but a brief conversation at the end of the lesson backed up by adequate written records will help to inform the teacher of pupil progress. Written records contain information that may be used to inform future planning. It is a good idea to involve TAs in this. When this is not possible, copies of the plans must be provided weekly for TAs.

● *Guidance on strategies to use with pupils*. Teachers and TAs working with SEN pupils must have knowledge of strategies and resources which will enable the pupil to have access to the curriculum.

● *Support and training*. Teachers should be advised on the most effective ways of working with TAs. This could be done by:
   ○ providing teachers with a selection of books to pick up ideas;
   ○ sharing ideas about best practice in relation to TAs;
   ○ inviting TAs to contribute their own ideas about ways in which they prefer to work with teachers.

● *Communication strategies*. These should ensure that TAs are fully informed both on aspects of school life directly relevant to their work and on broader issues. They could be:
   ○ provided with a copy of the minutes of the staff meetings;
   ○ encouraged to attend relevant training courses and given opportunities to feed back what they have learned to the staff;
   ○ encouraged to join a union, to ensure they are fully informed regarding all aspects of their role.

● *Extra paid time*. TAs should be paid to participate in meetings and whole-school activities. TAs attending after-school review meetings for SEN pupils should be compensated for their time, either through funding or by giving time off in lieu.

● *Funding for training*. Teachers and TAs should be given funding to participate in relevant training and development opportunities.

● *Appropriate accreditation and career structure*. TAs should be aware of their options and should be given relevant information and encouraged to undertake accredited courses.

● *Appropriate salary levels and structures*. These should recognise TAs' skills and expertise and reward them adequately.

The issues identified by Barbara Lee are important. Senior management, in their efforts to support their teachers and TAs working with pupils with SEN, must create a school environment that makes it possible to attain them.

Somebody else on the school team also plays a major role with regard to the support of pupils with SEN. I refer, of course, to the SENCo.

# Responsibilities of the SENCo

The SENCo usually acts as the line manager for teachers and TAs who are working with pupils placed at School Action Plus and statemented pupils. SENCos may find the following suggestions helpful to support them in their demanding role.

## Ten top tips

① **Hold regular meetings**

Organise regular meetings with teachers and TAs to discuss issues, to offer advice and support and to identify and resolve problems.

② **Ensure appropriate training**

Ensure teachers and TAs are offered adequate training, either by INSET provided within school or courses organised by the local education authority (LEA) or other providers. Discuss appropriate TA qualifications and find out what accredited courses the LEA are providing.

③ **Increase knowledge**

Gather information to increase knowledge of any difficulty experienced by a pupil and gain confidence in managing the situation. For example, if the SENCo has no prior experience of the problems associated with dyspraxia, they should collect articles about it and share the information gained with teachers and TAs. There are many useful and easily accessible associations, books and websites. Lists of these are given later in this book.

④ **Raise awareness of resources**

Raise awareness of SEN resources within the school and of how they can help. It would be useful to carry out an audit of existing resources and to order additional ones if required. They should be stored in an accessible place and labelled to indicate which area of the curriculum they cover. A meeting in the resource base should be arranged so the SENCo can indicate the uses of the resources to all the staff, including the TAs. These resources could then be included in the IEP information, which will provide a way for the SENCo to monitor their appropriateness.

⑤ **Monitor IEPs**

Monitor IEPs and ensure teachers and TAs are aware of useful strategies and techniques for use with particular pupils.

⑥ **Hold regular review meetings**

Hold regular review meetings at which teachers, TAs, parents and pupils can share in the discussion and target-setting process. Further information about reviews follows.

○ *Reviews for School Action pupils.* The progress of School Action pupils is usually reviewed termly. Ideally, these meetings should be attended by the SENCo, teacher, parent, pupil and TA involved – if there is one. Not all schools are able to allocate a TA to School Action pupils on a regular basis. Since reviews often take place after school and the TA may be involved with many School Action pupils, it may not be feasible to include them. Teachers should ask the TA for an informal written or verbal report to provide further information regarding the progress of the pupil for the meeting. The TA who cannot attend a review meeting should receive feedback from the teacher regarding the outcome of the review.

○ *Reviews for School Action Plus pupils.* Pupils whose needs are not adequately met at School Action go on to receive School Action Plus support, which may involve the intervention of an outside professional. Many schools will fund the services of a TA for School Action Plus pupils in order to deliver recommended programmes of work. At times, the LEA may provide early intervention funding if it is available; this means they will share the funding of a TA with the school for a specific period of time. The SENCo usually arranges these reviews with the visiting professional; again the teacher, TA, parents and pupil also need to be invited.

*'All teachers involved, as well as the SENCo, must study the statement carefully and understand the implications for them and their TA.'*

It may be necessary to request a statutory assessment, carried out by a multi-disciplinary team, to decide if the pupil needs the protection of a statement which recognises the fact that they have needs that cannot be met in the mainstream school without extra support. If the pupil is awarded a statement, the LEA will fund a specified number of hours weekly for a TA to work with them. All teachers involved, as well as the SENCo, must study the statement carefully and understand the implications for them and their TA.

○ *Reviews for pupils with statements.* The statement should be reviewed at least annually. The review meeting is usually arranged by the SENCo, and is an important part of the SEN process. The teacher and TA should always be invited to attend and should prepare a report. This will provide valuable information – along with all the other reports – to inform decisions about what happens next and what new targets should replace existing ones on the IEP.

SENCos may like to use the review meeting report sheet on page 13 with TAs. It provides a useful structure and guidelines, while ensuring a consistent approach is taken for report writing throughout the school. The report form may also be used for pupils at School Action and School Action Plus. An example of a completed report is given on page 12 as well as the blank photocopiable form for your own use.

# Review meeting report

## Example of completed report

**Name of pupil:** Mark Potter                                **Class:** Year 4

**Name of teaching assistant:** Barbara Cavanagh

**Weekly provision:** 4 hours (1 hour 1:1, 3 hours within small group)

**Date of review:** March 12th                        **Date report written:** March 5th

**IEP target:** To spell 10 identified words from NLS words

**Comment:** Mark is able to spell 7/10 words consistently, in and out of context.
He is unable to spell: should, about, because

**IEP target:** To learn the following consonant clusters: bl, fl, gl, pl, sl, br, cr, dr, fr, gr, pr, tr

**Comment:** Mark has achieved this target and also recognises sn, sp, sc, sl, sm, st, sw

**IEP target:** To be responsible for a daily task in class

**Comment:** Mark has done really well here. He takes the responsibility very seriously and always completes the set task. It has really helped his self-esteem.

### What has been positive about the support?

I enjoy working with Mark. Since he has been working with the group (one month) he has become more co-operative and now considers the needs and feelings of the other children.

### Is there anything you would like to change regarding the nature of the support?

No. He is making good progress the way things are and says he enjoys the sessions. I feel he needs the same amount of support at least until his next review.

### Do you have any further comments?

Yes. Mark's attitude to work has changed a lot since his last review. He puts more effort into his work and is beginning to make friends with the other children. He is much more confident, although he realises he still has a long way to go.

# Review meeting report

Name of pupil:                                    Class:

Name of teaching assistant:

Weekly provision:

Date of review:                                   Date report written:

IEP target:

Comment:

IEP target:

Comment:

IEP target:

Comment:

What has been positive about the support?

Is there anything you would like to change regarding the nature of the support?

Do you have any further comments?

© *How to support and teach children with special educational needs* LDA                Permission to Photocopy

⑦ **Raise awareness of medical conditions**

Ascertain that teachers and TAs know about any medical conditions experienced by pupils and know what to do in emergencies.

  ◗ Providing vital medical information. The government policy of inclusion – and the Special Educational Needs and Disability Act 2001 – mean that there are many pupils in our schools with medical needs and disabilities. Many schools have medical registers listing all pupils who experience some kind of medical problem. Frequently it is the SENCo who is given the responsibility for keeping this record. It should not be assumed that a pupil with a medical condition should also be regarded as having special educational needs; most of these pupils will not require special provision. The Code of Practice 2001 (Para. 7:64) states: 'A medical diagnosis or a disability does not necessarily imply SEN . . . It is the child's educational needs rather then a medical diagnosis that must be considered.' It is vital to obtain all the medical information necessary from parents, doctors and specialist services to ensure that the school provides a safe and effective environment. Schools need to take account of *Supporting Pupils with Medical Needs in School* (DfEE 1996). See also *Supporting Pupils with Medical Needs: A good practice guide* (DfEE/DoH 1996).

SENCos may find the form on page 16 useful in order to compile a medical information sheet for pupils. Copies for pupils with medical conditions in a particular class should be given to the class teacher. Additional copies should be provided for TAs. An example of a completed form is provided on page 15 as well as the blank copy.

⑧ **Encourage specialist learning**

Encourage TAs to become specialists in particular areas of SEN. When a TA is allocated a pupil experiencing a particular disability (hearing impairment, for example), opportunities to extend existing knowledge in that particular area should be offered by:

  ◗ encouraging attendance on relevant courses;
  ◗ recommending appropriate reading material;
  ◗ observing TAs in other schools in a similar situation.

Once a high level of skill is acquired, the TA could be employed when pupils with similar difficulties arrive in school. A further option may be to suggest a TA transfers to another school when pupils move there so the training and expertise are not wasted.

# Medical information form

Example of completed report

**Name of child:** Emma Smith          **Date of birth:** 06/02/95          **Class:** Year 4

**Teacher:** Mr Brown          **Teaching assistant:** Mrs Wingfield

**Medical condition:** Epilepsy

Emma suffers from generalised seizures. She may suddenly lose consciousness and fall to the ground. Her limbs will jerk and she may froth at the mouth. These episodes do not usually last long (sometimes a few seconds, rarely a few minutes) but may occur frequently. Her condition is largely controlled by her drugs, but these have side-effects and her ability to concentrate and remain focused is affected.

**What the teacher/teaching assistant needs to know:**

Emma should not be moved when she is unconscious unless she is in danger (for instance in a roadway). She needs to be in a safe environment so she comes to no physical harm. Clear the space around her. As soon as possible, turn her on her side in the recovery position and be calm and reassuring as she recovers consciousness as she tends to be confused and a little upset. It would be helpful if the other pupils were aware of Emma's condition and learnt to accept what happens without being afraid and to help in the best way they can – which means carrying on with what they are doing and not crowding around Emma.

**Prescribed medication:** Anti-epileptic drugs

**How often administered:** Once a day at lunchtime

**Named person in school:** Mrs Wingfield

**Possible side-effects:** Sleepiness

**Contact number in emergency (parent/carer):** 01777 653247 (Home number)

**Contact number in emergency (second contact):** 01777 665443 (Mr Smith, work)

**Name/phone number of doctor:** Dr Singh 01777 552552

**What school should do in an emergency:** If the seizure lasts more than a few minutes an ambulance should be called. Parents should be contacted.

# Medical information form

Name of child:                          Date of birth:                          Class:

Teacher:                                Teaching assistant:

Medical condition:



What the teacher/teaching assistant needs to know:



Prescribed medication:

How often administered:

Named person in school:

Possible side-effects:


Contact number in emergency (parent/carer):

Contact number in emergency (second contact):

Name/phone number of doctor:


What school should do in an emergency:

© How to support and teach children with special educational needs LDA          Permission to Photocopy

## ⑨ Monitor the TAs

Monitor the TAs by:

- observing them in the classroom situation (but it is rare for a SENCo to have an allocation of time which allows for this);
- regular discussion with class teachers;
- checking pupils' exercise books to observe progress and seek evidence that targets are being worked on and achieved.

A very useful way to simplify monitoring is to provide each TA who works with statemented pupils and pupils at School Action Plus with an SEN ring binder to store information. This will increase school efficiency and encourage good practice for the following people:

- *The SENCo*. An important part of the SENCo's role is to monitor the work of the TAs working with SEN pupils. Often time to observe and meet with TAs is limited. The ring binder offers an alternative way, by holding information provided on record sheets.
- *The teacher*. The information contained in the ring binder is also a useful resource for teachers since it offers detailed information regarding the pupil's progress. The teacher can regularly read through the record sheets, on which the TA notes the pupil's response in lessons. This information can be used to inform future planning regarding what the pupil should be doing – and consequently how the TA's time should be organised. It helps to compensate for the lack of time that teachers and TAs have for regular meetings. The records should not merely contain reports on work completed, but should also be a reflection of other issues which may impact on the pupil's progress (see left). These are issues which teachers need to raise with parents to see if these situations can be resolved. We can't teach Halina if she can't see properly, Jimmy if he can't keep awake, Chendu if he hasn't completed his homework to consolidate the previous day's input, or Angela if she is hungry.

It is very important that TAs keep records of their pupil's work. These records are important for several reasons:

- to provide information for the teacher regarding the progress of the child/children which can be used in weekly planning;
- to remind the TA of what aspects of the work need consolidation;
- to refer to when writing the review report;
- to provide evidence of incidents that may be relevant – the pupil is always upset on Tuesdays, for example;
- to provide evidence if needed for child protection case conferences;
- to provide evidence for the SENCo when monitoring the effectiveness of the TA.

The record sheet on page 19 may be used by TAs who work with School Action Plus and statemented pupils. A completed example precedes the record sheet.

### Notes from a ring binder

*Jimmy was very tired again this morning and said he was watching videos very late.*

*Halina forgot her glasses again, so she was unable to read her book.*

*Chendu did not bring his homework in again. He said there is no place for him to do it at home.*

*Angela was very hungry this morning, as she did not have any breakfast. I gave her some biscuits and then she settled down to work.*

# Record sheet for teaching assistants

Example of completed report

**Teacher:** Mr Gibson

**Class:** 4

| Date | Activity/target/resources | Observations | Target achieved? |
|---|---|---|---|
| 12/04/04 | **Writing**<br>To write one sentence independently. Completing pages 5–6 Easylearn 'Single Sentences'. Arranging word cards into correct order and copying the sentence. | Max completed all the activities and used a capital letter when he wrote out the sentence. | Yes, but needs more practice. |
| 13/04/04 | **Phonics**<br>To be able to cvc blend consistently. Phonics tape: Breaking the Code and completing the worksheets (page 7). | Max did not have time to complete the worksheet. He found it difficult to stay on task today. He was in the same mood last week too. Aims to complete work next time. | No |
| 14/04/04 | **Maths**<br>To learn number bonds to 10 using plasticine balls. | Max still finds this very difficult. Need to find another way to get this over. | No |
| 15/04/04 | **Writing**<br>To write one sentence independently, using word cards. | Max was able to produce and write several sentences on his own. Am really pleased with him. | Yes! |

**Name of pupil:** Max Fefhega     **Name of teaching assistant:** Helen Charles

© How to support and teach children with special educational needs LDA

Permission to Photocopy

# Record sheet for teaching assistants

Teacher: _____

Class: _____

| Date | Activity/target/resources | Observations | Target achieved? |
|------|---------------------------|--------------|------------------|
|      |                           |              |                  |

Name of pupil: _____

Name of teaching assistant: _____

© How to support and teach children with special educational needs LDA     Permission to Photocopy

Continuing on, the ring binder will also be useful for:

○ *The teaching assistant.* The ring binder is an invaluable resource for the TAs themselves, since it enables all the information regarding their specific pupils to be located in one place. Details of progress, review information, samples of work to provide evidence of the progress of the pupil, and newspaper articles offering additional information about the pupil's difficulties – all this helps to keep them focused.

The binder is also invaluable if TAs are absent from school over a prolonged period of time. The detailed information enables a replacement to become quickly familiar with the needs of the pupil in question.

○ *The Local Education Authority.* The LEA provides funding for TAs who work with pupils with statements. The ring binder provides comprehensive evidence of the pupil's progress, and demonstrates how efficiently the school is using the services of the TA.

○ *OFSTED.* The ring binder information is useful for any inspector, since it provides details of the support the pupil has received, sometimes over a prolonged period. It also offers work samples which illustrate the progress of the pupils and demonstrate the effectiveness of the TA's support.

○ *Parents.* It is reassuring for parents to have occasional access to the ring binder so they may observe the details and quality of the support offered to their child. Sometimes the information provided is tangible evidence of issues that are the responsibilities of parents, which may be contributing to the pupil's lack of achievement in school.

○ *The pupils.* The existence of the ring binder is important to the pupil because it constitutes a methodical and well-organised way of recording progress and updating assessment on their behalf. The pupil could be asked to provide samples of work to be kept in the folder to demonstrate:

  ○ visual proof of the progress they are making;
  ○ evidence that IEP targets have been achieved (such as spelling tests, pieces of completed writing, photocopies of maths work).

An outline of the possible contents of the ring binder appears on page 21. SENCos may wish to alter these to suit their own situation.

### ⑩ Look after yourself

The most important tip of all is that it is important for SENCos to ensure they are well looked after themselves. They will need time, training, funds and resources if they are to succeed. It is important to feel part of a group, and to know they are not the only one struggling with the increasing demands and complexities of the role.

SENCos will often find problems arising which they have not encountered before. Further advice and support may be found on the website for SENCos (SENCo Forum) which is co-ordinated by the British Educational and Technology Communications Agency (BECTA; see References, page 64).

**Teaching assistant's SEN ring binder**

Section 1:
Copy of timetable indicating how and where the allocated hours are spent.

Section 2:
Copy of current IEP (if the TA is employed to support more than one pupil there may be additional IEPs).

Section 3:
Completed record sheets for individual pupils (example on page 18).

Section 4:
Completed review reports (example on page 12).

Section 5:
Assessment information provided by the school.
Checklists for reading/spelling/numeracy.
Checklists to identify pupils with special educational needs (pages 55–62).

Section 6:
Paperwork blanks.
Record sheets (see page 19).
Review sheets (see page 13).

Section 7:
Any useful additional information; for example if the pupil being supported has Asperger Syndrome, it would be useful to store this information here for reference. The extra information may simply be a booklist, a website or articles from newspapers and magazines.

Section 8:
Significant samples of pupil's work; for example a sample of mirror writing completed by a dyslexic pupil may be useful evidence of the complexity of the problem. Additional work samples to provide evidence of pupil progress (or lack of it) over a period of time.

We now move onto the next crucial part of the process: the responsibilities of the teacher.

LEEDS COLLEGE OF BUILDING
LIBRARY

# Responsibilities of the teacher

An important task for any teacher is, of course, to identify the fact that a child has an SEN in the first place. The services of a TA may be introduced to support the identification and to provide evidence to confirm the teacher's initial concern. To make clear what is meant by the term 'special educational need', we quote from the 2001 SEN Code of Practice (Para. 1:3):

> Children have special educational needs if they have a learning difficulty which calls for special educational provision to be made for them.
> Children have a learning difficulty if they:
> (a) have a significantly greater difficulty in learning than the majority of children of the same age; or
> (b) have a disability which prevents or hinders them from making use of educational facilities of a kind generally provided for children of the same age in schools within the area of the local education authority
> (c) are under compulsory school age and fall within the definition at (a) or (b) above or would so do if special educational provision was not made for them.

*'An important task for any teacher is, of course, to identify the fact that a child has an SEN in the first place.'*

> Children must not be regarded as having a learning difficulty solely because the language or form of language of their home is different from the language in which they will be taught.

The Code emphasises there are no 'hard and fast categories of special educational need' (Para. 7:52). Instead, it recognises the uniqueness of every child, and prefers to identify areas of need. These relate to:

- communication and interaction;
- cognition and learning;
- behavioural, emotional and social development;
- sensory and/or physical needs;
- medical conditions.

## Initial identification of a special educational need

The initial identification of an SEN may have occurred before the child attends school, and a statement may already have been awarded. When this is the case, the school needs to prepare for the arrival of the child, ensuring all the necessary equipment and resources are ready and liaison with the professional involved has taken place. The school should also have recruited a TA to work with the child. It is helpful if the TA can meet the pupil before school begins.

The special needs of most pupils, however, will be identified after they start school. It may be some time before the educational need becomes obvious. Teachers in all key stages must be vigilant in their scrutiny of pupils who have not, as yet, been identified because:

- the need may have only recently developed;
- the need was not apparent before the child entered school;

❍ the pupil had attended many schools and there had been insufficient time for any of these schools to make arrangements to acknowledge the need;

❍ the situation has not been acknowledged or recognised previously;

❍ the situation has been wrongly diagnosed – for example, an ADHD pupil has been labelled as 'naughty'.

TAs can help teachers with the identification of such pupils. Once a teacher expresses a concern and needs further information regarding the pupil's situation, it is important, after consultation with the SENCo, to provide further evidence to clarify the initial concern. This may be achieved by making use of the checklists provided in this book (see Appendix, pages 55–62). These checklists are to be used to clarify a child's difficulties, after which further assessment may be required. The TA could administer the checklists daily over a period of specified time, after which the results are analysed to see if further action should be taken.

The checklists represent the various areas recognised by the SEN Code of Practice and also serve to raise the awareness of both teachers and TAs regarding indicators of the range of difficulties associated with pupils with SEN. This information will help prevent pupils at risk slipping through the net. It is distressing to discover pupils occasionally who have entered secondary education with an SEN that had not been identified previously, and which may have contributed to all kinds of difficulties within school – including learning, social and emotional problems. If the child has been given appropriate support some of these problems might have been modified or resolved.

The checklists cover the following areas of need:
❍ Speech and language difficulties
❍ Autistic spectrum disorder/Asperger Syndrome
❍ General learning difficulties
❍ Dyslexia
❍ Dyspraxia
❍ Behavioural, emotional and social difficulties
❍ Hearing impairment
❍ Visual impairment.

The checklist for pupils with autism refers to the criteria to identify pupils with Asperger Syndrome; it is these pupils, not usually those given the diagnosis of 'high functioning autism', who are likely to be included within mainstream schools.

Once identification has been made, increased differentiation of the curriculum is needed. If this proves insufficient, further action will need to be taken and the pupil is placed at School Action.

## The teacher and School Action pupils

Appropriate targets should be identified on an IEP. Many teachers will use the services of TAs to support pupils in reaching those targets. They may sit with groups of School Action pupils in literacy and numeracy sessions, for example, offering hands-on support, or work with School Action pupils in order to deliver specific programmes of work.

The school may decide pupils with literacy problems will benefit from a second-chance reading scheme – such as Wellington Square, or Fuzz Buzz – and allocate TA time to facilitate the delivery of the programme.

The DfES *Teaching Assistant File* issued in September 2002 for use in initial training for TAs offers some good ideas for supporting pupils in the Literacy Hour:

- drawing in reticent pupils – these pupils are too timid to put their hands up;
- starting the ball rolling when pupils are slow to start a discussion;
- supportive behaviour to less able or less confident pupils;
- joining in and making contributions;
- demonstrating for the teacher;
- acting as devil's advocate;
- echoing the teacher by repeating or rewording phrases for puils who may need help;
- acting as an extra pair of eyes;
- assisting with behaviour management;
- resource management.

## The teacher and School Action Plus pupils

Pupils who fail to make adequate progress at School Action are likely to move on to support at School Action Plus, which may mean the teacher has the assistance of a professional employed by the LEA.

The teacher, in co-operation with the professional, will decide on appropriate IEP targets and how to make the most efficient use of the TA's time. Schools may be able to offer some individual TA support to these pupils or they may still be supported mainly within a group.

## The teacher and pupils with statements

If, following a period of statutory assessment, the LEA recognise that the pupil has needs which cannot be met in the mainstream without extra support, a specified number of hours weekly will be funded for a TA to work with a pupil. It is essential that teachers, as well as the SENCo, study the statement carefully and understand the implications for them and their TAs. The teacher should be supported by the SENCo when devising the IEP targets.

'The teacher, in co-operation with the professional, will decide on appropriate IEP targets and how to make the most efficient use of the TA's time.'

It would be useful for teachers to seek as much information as possible, in addition to that provided by any visiting professional and the SENCo, to increase their knowledge of the needs of their pupils.

We have so far looked at the different roles those working with children with special needs have in relation to each other and to the children in their care.

Part 2 aims to provide additional knowledge and also useful, practical strategies and tips to ensure the needs of pupils with SEN are being met as effectively as possible. The teacher needs to feel confident that their approach to particular pupils is appropriate and that they can offer positive support and direction to TAs.

# Part 2
# Strategies for support

Pupils experiencing difficulties are likely to have problems within one, or more, of the areas of special needs identified in the SEN Code of Practice. We shall look at each of these in turn.

## Major sources of help

In each of the areas of special needs identified in this book there are a number of sources of help for the teacher and the TA. Three particular ones relate to all the areas. What they will do to help is explained in this section.

- ❍ Educational psychologists, who may be able to offer the following support:
  - ❍ training for all staff;
  - ❍ working with parents;
  - ❍ demonstrating various techniques and resources to teachers and TAs;
  - ❍ assessing individual children, maybe as part of the statutory assessment procedure to decide if the child needs the protection of a statement;
  - ❍ advice on ways of differentiating the curriculum;
  - ❍ advice on the delivery of specific work programmes, resources and general classroom organisation.
- ❍ Specialist teachers employed by the LEA, who have experience and expertise in a particular area. They may work in school for a specified period of time with the child, or act in a monitoring capacity. They should be available to assist with IEP targets and resources, and to give advice and training to teachers and TAs.
- ❍ Parents, who may co-operate with any out-of-school appointments, work on any IEP targets at home, assist with homework, attend review meetings and inform the school of any problems which occur at home.

## Communication and interaction difficulties

The problems experienced by pupils in this area are wide ranging. Some experience difficulties with speech, language or communication or all three. Their problems may be mild, or complex and severe. These pupils include those who demonstrate features within the autistic spectrum.

### Speech and language difficulties

Pupils with speech and language difficulties experience a wide range of problems, from relatively minor speech impairments to specific complex disorders. Problems may involve their receptive vocabulary and their ability to understand what other people are saying, such as instructions. They may fail to understand the meaning of words or the meaning behind the words – leading to difficulty with sarcasm, social expectation, disapproval and humour. Others have expressive language difficulties: they will have a problem with making other people understand what they are saying. They may not speak clearly or they may lack the ability to produce words or express their thoughts, and they may have a problem with sequencing thoughts into words to form sentences. Children with speech problems may not be able to articulate certain words.

## Strategies for teachers

- ⊙ Remind pupils to listen at regular intervals.
- ⊙ Keep instructions precise and clear.
- ⊙ Check that the pupil has understood through questioning and discussion.
- ⊙ Check understanding by asking the pupil what they have learnt from the story or the instruction that has been given.
- ⊙ Give the pupil extra time to listen and respond.
- ⊙ Use repetition and demonstration.
- ⊙ Use words that the child will understand.
- ⊙ Produce word lists showing the meaning of words and display them around the classroom.
- ⊙ Explain the meaning of new words.
- ⊙ Reward the child when they have listened or followed instructions. For example, 'Well done, Jasminder. You listened carefully and have been able to answer an important question. Now you can choose someone to answer the next question. Who will it be?'
- ⊙ Make eye contact and use non-verbal cues to emphasise important points.

## How teaching assistants can help

- ⊙ Administer the checklist as a means of gathering evidence (see page 55).
- ⊙ Carry out programmes designed by a speech and language therapist. These will be recommended following thorough assessment, and may include practising certain sounds or undertaking work to develop comprehension.

- ⊙ Use ICT as a means of encouraging non-verbal expression. When verbal expression is difficult, pupils may learn to express themselves successfully in a written form. Teaching keyboard skills is important, particularly if fine motor skills also present problems. A useful programme to teach these skills is Typequick for Students (see page 28).
- ⊙ Keep a watchful eye to ensure the child does not become isolated because of difficulties with verbal communication.
- ⊙ Introduce new vocabulary in advance whenever possible (pre-tutoring).
- ⊙ Support the pupil in literacy and numeracy lessons as follows:
  - ⊙ Sitting near the pupil to offer support and encouragement.
  - ⊙ Encouraging the pupil to offer verbal contributions. 'Hey, Inez, you know the answer to that. Put your hand up!'
  - ⊙ Sharing books to encourage the pupil to respond verbally.
  - ⊙ Acting as spokesperson for the pupil at appropriate times. 'John has written a really good description – shall I read it to the class, John?'

○ Ensuring the pupil is included in discussion within the peer group by observing the pupils' interaction and prompting occasionally, perhaps by asking a question: 'What do you think about what Jason just said, Peter? Do you think it is cruel to keep animals in a zoo?'

○ Keeping records of the child's progress to assist the teacher with weekly planning and differentiation.

○ Repeating back to the child words they have said that do not appear to make sense. 'Have I got this right, Meena? You said you wanted to play with the sand? No? Show me then. Oh, you want to play with the soldiers. I see.'

○ Repeating back to the child words they have said that do make sense: 'You said you want an apple. Well done. Here you are.'

## Additional support

○ Educational psychologists (see page 26).

○ Speech and language therapists, who may require the child to be taken to clinics in or out of school hours. They may also provide training for teachers and TAs.

○ A speech and language unit where pupils may spend a brief period undergoing intensive therapy before returning to school.

○ Parents (see page 26).

○ Neurologists, who may be involved in determining a possible physical cause for the speech and/or language difficulty.

## Useful books
*Teaching Children with Speech and Language Difficulties,* Deirdre Martin in association with the School of Education, University of Birmingham. David Fulton, 2000

*Speech and Language Difficulties* (Spotlight on Special Educational Needs), Bob Daines, Pam Fleming and Carol Miller. NASEN, 2003

*How to Identify and Support Children with Speech and Language Difficulties,* Jane Speake. LDA, 2003

## Useful resource
*Typequick for Students,*
Iansyst Ltd

## *Autistic spectrum disorders*
Some pupils have problems with communication that are complex and severe. These include children on the autistic spectrum. Pupils with autism are likely to have been identified before school age. They will usually enter school with the protection of a statement and have TA time allocated to them.

**Useful addresses and websites**

Afasic
2nd Floor, 50–52 Great Sutton Street,
London EC1V ODJ
Tel.: 020 7490 9410
Helpline: 0845 355 5577
*www.afasic.org.uk*

I Can
4 Dyer's Buildings, Holborn,
London EC1N 2QP
Tel.: 0845 225 4071
*www.ican.org.uk*

The National Autistic Society describes autism in the following way:

> People with autism are not physically disabled in the same way that a person with cerebral palsy may be. They do not require wheelchairs and they look just like anybody without a disability. Due to this invisible nature it can be much harder to create awareness and understanding of the condition. Autism is a lifelong developmental disability that affects the way a person relates and communicates with people around them. Children and adults have difficulty relating to others in a meaningful way. They can have accompanying learning disabilities but everyone with the condition shares a difficulty in making sense of the world.

## Asperger Syndrome

In 1944, Hans Asperger recognised a group of children who had higher levels of intelligence and linguistic ability than other autistic children, but there are many similarities between the way these children respond to life and the way autistic children respond. The National Autistic Society describes Asperger Syndrome as follows:

> It is a form of autism, a condition that affects the way a person communicates and relates to others. However, people with Asperger syndrome usually have fewer problems with language than those with autism, often speaking fluently, though their words can sometimes appear formal or stilted. They do not usually have learning difficulties and are often of average or above average intelligence.

## Strategies for teachers

- Point out pupils who are already following instructions, for example sitting quietly in order to clarify what it is you want them to do.
- Provide opportunities for playing games with other children, but avoid competitive games, which may cause confusion. Games that encourage the idea of taking turns can be useful.
- Demonstrate how a game is played as well as giving instructions.
- Encourage other children to act as befrienders.
- Enrol suitable pupils to act as carers who will invite them to join in playtime games or sit next to them at lunch.
- Make sure your instructions are clear and check understanding by providing the child with checklists. An example is supplied.

> **Checklist**
> *When I go into class I hang my coat up.*
> *Then I go and sit at my table.*
> *I take out my pencil and I write neatly in my book.*
> *I put my hand up when I want to ask a question.*

- Back up oral instructions with writing or drawing.
- Cut down on unnecessary distractions.

- Build on the child's strengths and interests.
- Talk about others' thoughts and feelings in circle time.
- Warn and explain to them any change in routines, perhaps by the provision of a visual timetable.

### Visual timetable

- Organise resources to ensure skills are learned in context. Autistic pupils have difficulty in generalising learning. For example, use real money in a real shopping experience; a school tuck shop would be ideal.

## How the teaching assistant can help

- Administer the checklist as a means of gathering evidence (see page 56).
- Ensure the pupil is sitting in a position in which they feel comfortable. They may need to sit always in the same place, or to be seated well away from the door – which may create a distraction.
- Escort the pupil from the classroom to a quiet place if they become agitated or upset. They may become distressed if their regular teacher is away or there is a sudden change in the timetable. A brief time out of the classroom may help them to come to terms with the change.
- Adapt language to ensure the pupil understands. For example, instead of saying in numeracy, 'Get your books out', give more detail: 'Get your *blue* maths book out.'
- Do not put pressure on the pupil to maintain eye contact, but do encourage it. The pupil has to learn to recognise what behaviour is acceptable in the world beyond school, when not everyone will be aware of their condition – and if they are, they may not have sympathy with it.
- Teach the pupil to recognise non-verbal signals – for example when it is the right time to settle down and listen to the teacher.
- Be vigilant in meeting the child's needs. Can they see the teacher? Are they distracted by work going on outside? Are they unable to concentrate because the light of the sun reflected on the wall has gained their attention?
- Work with the child in a distraction-free zone at times when they need to concentrate. This zone may be created within the classroom by using a display screen to cordon off a quiet area.
- Ensure the pupil knows where all necessary resources are kept and that they are returned to the place where they are always kept after use.
- Teach the child social skills by pointing out what other children are doing. Persuade pupils to participate in circle time activities. Encourage pupils to imitate other pupils when appropriate. 'Oh look, Mandy is changing her shoes. Can you do that?'

"Ensure the pupil is sitting in a position in which they feel comfortable."

**Useful addresses and websites**
National Autistic Society Headquarters
393 City Road, London EC1V 1NG
Tel.: 020 7833 2299
*www.nas.org.uk*

Allergy Induced Autism
11 Larklands, Peterborough PE3 6LL
Tel.: 01733 331771
*www.autismmedical.com*

Autism File
Tel.: 020 8979 2525
*www.autismfile.com*

This website provides information on a
wide range of available resources
*www.autism-resources.com*

○ Keep records of the child's progress to assist the teacher with weekly planning and differentiation.

○ Monitor obsessional behaviour and seek advice about minimising it or replacing obstructive obsessions with less intrusive ones.

## Additional help

○ Educational psychologists (see page 26).

○ Specialist teachers (see page 26).

○ School medical officer, who may be involved as part of a multi-professional diagnosis.

○ Parents (see page 26).

## Useful books

*Supporting Communication Disorders: A handbook for teachers and teaching assistants*, Gill Thompson. David Fulton, 2003

*Understanding and Teaching Children with Autism*, Rita Jordan and Stuart Powell. John Wiley and Sons, 1995

*The Autistic Spectrum: A guide for parents and professionals*, Lorna Wing. Constable and Robinson, 2003

*Martian in the Playground: Understanding the schoolchild with Asperger's syndrome*, Clare Sainsbury. Lucky Duck Publishing Ltd, 2000

Food for thought
*Mind Blind*

If I told you she was blind
you'd see part of what I meant

If I told you she was deaf
you'd hear something of what I said

If I told you she couldn't walk
you'd meet us halfway

But what if I told you she looks
straight at me yet can't see me?

She hears what I say but
doesn't know I'm talking
She walks beside me but
doesn't know I'm there

She doesn't know
that when the corners of my
mouth turn up I'm happy

That's when water runs from
my eyes, I'm sad

She doesn't know
That if she spoke I'd listen
if she told me where it hurts
I'd kiss it better.

She's mind blind you see.

I know it's hard to believe and
even harder to understand.
But every time you try
she comes a little closer.

© *John Burns*, Wind Dancer:
Autism, A Father's poems *(Wendy Webb Books, Norwich 2001)*

# Cognition and learning difficulties

The Code of Practice identifies as a distinct area problems associated with pupils facing cognition and learning difficulties. The level and complexity of difficulty varies. For pupils who experience mild learning difficulties, a catch-up programme, often administered by a TA, may meet their needs. Their SEN may be only temporary. Other pupils have complex and far-ranging needs. These include specific learning difficulties such as dyslexia and dyspraxia, and problems of a more general nature, as outlined below.

## *General learning difficulties*

Pupils with general learning difficulties can usually be recognised by their inability to meet the desired standards in school, in particular the appropriate level identified in the National Curriculum. They may also have problems in acquiring literacy or numeracy skills or both, and experience difficulty with the acquisition of abstract ideas and in generalising from experience.

### Strategies for teachers

- Simplify language, repeat words, clarify meaning.

- Be aware of the pupil's preferred learning style and differentiate all work accordingly. It may be helpful to assess the learning styles of all your pupils to ensure they have appropriate access to the curriculum. A suitable test is to be found in Smith (1996), which also contains information about how you can adapt your teaching to take account of learning styles. Encourage the child to respond to set work in ways appropriate to their preferred learning style – drawing a picture, using the computer, making models, participating in role play and so on.

- Teach the same concept in a variety of ways using a multi-sensory approach. Ensure that resources are available to work with visual learners (books, diagrams, videos), auditory learners (create opportunities for discussion and listening to audio tapes) and kinaesthetic learners (who learn best through 'feeling and doing'). These children will benefit from practical activities such as playing games or role play, and will need regular opportunities to move around in order to keep them on task. Playing music can help.

- Allow time for frequent repetition, for example when the children are learning spellings and tables. The use of a programme of precision teaching, in which a pupil is invited to read as many words as they can within a specified time, may be useful. For further details of this type of programme contact the Sandwell Child Psychology Service (see page 33).

- Adapt worksheets to enable the pupil to understand the work.

- Keep records of the child's progress to assist with weekly planning and differentiation.

- Ensure the pupil's needs are fully assessed and that the targets on the IEP are appropriate.

- Introduce resources which are appropriate and will provide access to learning.

**Useful addresses and websites**

Sandwell Child Psychology Service
Tel.: 0121 569 2200

SENJIT: Special Educational Needs
Joint Initiative for Training
*www.ioe.ac.uk/senjit*

NASEN: a support group which offers
information and advice
*www.nasen.org.uk*

National Curriculum guidelines for
inclusion
*www.nc.uk.net/inclusion*

QCA website which provides
information to ensure education can
include all learners
*www.qca.org.uk/ca/inclusion*

An excellent source of useful links
*www.teacherxpress.com*

◗ Make sure strategies are in place for raising self-esteem – ensure that there are areas in which the pupil can succeed. Work targets need to be realistic and achievable. The use of circle time can help.

◗ Ensure that lesson plans include suitably differentiated work.

◗ Differentiate the questions in question-and-answer sessions.

## How the teaching assistant can help

◗ Administer the checklist as a means of gathering evidence (see page 57).

◗ Complete on-going assessments, such as updating the pupil's progress in acquiring sight and spelling words, by completing tick boxes.

◗ Administer particular programmes of work, such as a second-chance reading scheme – Wellington Square or Fuzz Buzz, for example – or completing a programme to develop the pupil's phonological awareness, such as the PAT scheme (see References, page 64).

◗ Work in a one-to-one situation or with small groups to offer consolidation and support.

◗ Keep ongoing records to inform teachers of areas of difficulty so they can pay attention to these in their planning.

## Additional help

◗ Educational psychologists (see page 26).

◗ Specialist teachers (see page 26).

◗ Parents (see page 26).

Food for thought

(I wonder why more of us don't have a spelling difficulty?)

*Spelling*

If an S and an I and an O and a U with an X at the end spells Sioux,
And an E and a Y and an E spells eye;
If an S and an I and a G and an H and an E and a D spells sighed,
Pray what is there left for a speller to do but –
To go and commit Sioux-eye-sighed?

*Anonymous,* The Kingfisher Book of Comic Verse, *ed. Roger McGough, 1991*

## Useful books
*Learning Difficulties* (Spotlight on Special Educational Needs), Sally Beveridge. NASEN, 1996

*Pupils with Learning Difficulties in Mainstream Schools,* Christina Tilstone, Penny Lacey, Jill Porter and Christopher Robertson. David Fulton, 1999

*Pupils with Complex Learning Difficulties: Promoting learning using visual materials and methods,* Dr Jill Porter and Rob Ashdown. NASEN, 2002

LEEDS COLLEGE OF BUILDING
LIBRARY

Having looked at general learning difficulties, we now turn to specific difficulties.

## Dyslexia

The Dyslexia Institute gives the following explanation of this condition:

> Dyslexia is a specific learning difficulty that hinders the learning of literacy skills. The problem with managing verbal codes in memory is neurologically based and tends to run in families. Other symbolic systems, such as mathematics and musical notation, can also be affected. Dyslexia can occur at any level of intellectual ability. It can accompany, but is not the result of, lack of motivation, emotional disturbance, sensory impairment, or meagre opportunities. The effects of dyslexia can be alleviated by skilled specialist teaching and committed learning.

### Strategies for teachers

- Discuss with the pupil what approaches seem to help. Ask them if they have a seating preference, whether they would enjoy reading with a reading buddy, if they are able to copy from the board or would be more comfortable copying from a near model in front of them.
- Acknowledge the effort made, not the content.
- Accept alternative forms of recording that will allow the child to reflect their true potential and understanding. For example, use diagrams, pictures, paired work, group scribing, taping, keyboard.
- Mark written work for the content and level of understanding.
- Focus on specific key words for the child to correct and learn. Do not overload them with corrections. Have an agreement with the pupil that you will pick up on a certain amount of spellings – maybe three or four.
- Discuss ways of remembering words by looking at their visual appearance, shape, beginning and ending.
- Assist with recording by providing subject-specific word cards or developing a bank of key words for pupil reference. These could be displayed on the classroom wall or on a bookmark, or a word bank could be prepared in advance of a lesson with tricky words that are likely to be needed already in place. Additional spellings may be added as the lesson progresses.
- Allow the child extra time to make written responses.
- Encourage the use of a spell checker.
- Keep instructions short and make sure they are well sequenced.
- Provide structured aids for organisation – a clear timetable, systems for providing appropriate equipment in case they forget.
- Encourage the use of memory aids to assist with spelling.
- Have high expectations of success and a positive approach.
- Explore which paper is most suitable – some pupils need to work on coloured paper with coloured pens as they may experience visual

*For me one of the things which helped me was having my problem taken seriously by people who really understood it.*

*From* Let's Discuss Dyslexia and Associated Difficulties, *by Pete Sanders and Steve Myers (Franklin Watts, 1995)*

**Useful addresses and websites**

British Dyslexia Association
98 London Road, Reading,
Berkshire RG1 5AU
Tel.: 0118 966 8271
*www.bdadyslexia.org.uk*

Dyslexia Action
Park House, Wick Road, Egham,
Surrey TW20 0HH
Tel.: 01784 222300
*www.dyslexiaaction.org.uk*

Dyslexia Inspirations
PO Box 243, Swansea SA3 1YA
Tel.: 01792 390 625
*www.dyslexia-inspirations.com*

There is an internet forum available for
students with dyslexia
*www.dyslexia-net.co.uk*

discomfort, text distortion and headaches when confronted by black print on white paper.

○ The use of overlays may help some pupils.

## How teaching assistants can help

○ Administer the checklist as a means of gathering evidence (see page 58).

○ Administer specifically designed programmes recommended by the LEA specialist or class teacher – for example Active Literacy Kit, Number Shark, Word Shark (see page 36).

○ Test progress in order to monitor or establish a starting point for a particular programme of work – for example known sight words, phonics, spellings.

○ Give support in class across the curriculum to enable the pupil to have access to subject-matter by using appropriate differentiated resources – for example worksheets with cloze procedure activities.

○ Read maths problems together to enable the pupil to complete the work.

○ Act as a scribe in test situations and in lessons, where appropriate.

○ Offer praise and encouragement to help pupils stay on task.

○ Teach keyboard skills under the direction of a specialist teacher. An example is Typequick for Students (see page 28).

○ Practise daily spellings to reinforce the spelling programme.

○ Practise handwriting daily to establish cursive script and correct letter and number formation.

○ Practise common sequences – days of the week, months of the year, for instance – using word cards, sequencing cards, and rhyming jingles such as 'Solomon Grundy, born on a Monday'.

○ Encourage organisational skills – ask the pupil to complete a checklist for each day to ensure they have all the equipment they need at the start of lessons.

○ Improve auditory memory by asking the pupil to repeat instructions.

○ Ensure the board can be seen adequately; pupils will find copying difficult.

○ Keep records of the child's progress to assist the teacher with weekly planning and differentiation.

Food for thought

Yvonne: parent of a dyslexic child

It was absolutely heartbreaking. I felt I was committing child abuse sending her to school. Eventually she would get to sleep, but often woke up again in the middle of the night, with nightmares. Sometimes she would wet the bed, and in the mornings the whole process would begin again – the white face, the 'I've got a headache, 'I don't feel well' . . .

*From* The Reality of Dyslexia, *by John Osmond (Brookline Books, 1999)*

## Additional help

- ⊙ Educational psychologists (see page 26).
- ⊙ Specialist teachers (see page 26).
- ⊙ Parents (see page 26).

## Useful books

*The Dyslexia Handbook,* J. Crisfield. The British Dyslexia Association, 2003

*Overcoming Dyslexia: A straightforward guide for families and teachers,* B. Hornsby. Vermilion, 1996

*How to Identify and Support Children with Dyslexia,* Chris Neanon. LDA, 2002

*How to Develop Numeracy in Children with Dyslexia,* Pauline Clayton. LDA, 2003

## Useful resources

*Active Literacy Kit, Number Shark, Word Shark, Beat Dyslexia*
All available from LDA

## *Dyscalculia*

Teachers and TAs need to have some knowledge of another specific learning difficulty, known as dyscalculia. It closely parallels dyslexia, but not all pupils with dyscalculia have dyslexia. The main criterion is a distinct discrepancy between a child's maths ability and their general ability.

Dyscalculia is recognised when pupils have problems with the following:
- ⊙ Counting forwards and backwards.
- ⊙ Memorising and using multiplication tables.
- ⊙ Reversing numbers – 31 for 13, for example.
- ⊙ Telling the time.
- ⊙ Understanding mathematical signs and words such as *add*, *subtract*, *divide* and *multiply*.
- ⊙ Mental arithmetic.

### Useful books and websites

The websites and books referred to in the section on dyslexia (see page 35) will be useful to teachers requiring further information and advice on dyscalculia. In addition, the following book is recommended:

*Specific Learning Difficulties in Mathematics: A classroom approach,* Olwen El-Naggar. NASEN, 1996

## Strategies for teachers and teaching assistants

- ⊙ Allow extra time for completion of work.
- ⊙ Take a multi-sensory approach: encourage the pupil to visualise the maths problems, draw a picture to aid understanding and then allow the child to explain what they have just learned.
- ⊙ Use repetition, rhyme and music to help with memorising tables and facts.
- ⊙ Ensure worksheets are simple.
- ⊙ Encourage the pupil to read the problem, or have it read to them.
- ⊙ Work with real-life situations whenever possible – for example the school tuck shop, collecting in money for school trips.

## *Dyspraxia*

The definition of dyspraxia used by the Dyspraxia Foundation is as follows:

> An impairment or immaturity of the organisation of movement, and in many individuals there may be associated problems with language, perception and thought.

It is thought that one in ten of the population may be affected by the condition, which is sometimes known as developmental dyspraxia or developmental co-ordination disorder (DCD). Children with dyspraxia will have particular difficulty with numeracy, reading, physical education and handwriting.

### Strategies for teachers

- Offer lots of praise and encouragement.
- Provide an area of responsibility: giving out books, taking the register to the office or delivering messages around the school, for example.
- Involve the pupil in group activities to encourage co-operative work.
- Make sure the pupil sticks to the classroom rules and is frequently reminded what they are.
- Provide the pupil with a sloping desk top if it helps.
- Use wide-lined exercise books when necessary to allow for large-scale writing.
- Include the use of diagrams or charts as part of the lesson to facilitate understanding.
- Introduce joined writing as early as possible to develop fluency and spaces between words. A handwriting programme based on a kinaesthetic approach, such as *Write from the Start* (see page 38), will help to develop motor skills.
- Have concrete materials such as counting rods and abacuses to help with numeracy.
- Allow more time before and after physical education lessons for the child to get ready.
- Try to reduce distractions in the class when giving instructions and make sure instructions and sequences are presented a little at a time.

### How teaching assistants can help

- Administer the checklist as a means of gathering evidence (see page 59).
- Oversee the daily exercise programme recommended by the occupational therapist and/or physiotherapist if appropriate.
- Use symbols or pictures to facilitate understanding and establish key points. For example prepare a visual timetable, or work with sequencing cards prior to story-writing activities.
- Act as a scribe for the pupil when appropriate.
- Use a tape recorder with the pupil and write down what was said later.

○ Encourage the use of a computer whenever possible, to enable the pupil to produce attractively presented and legible work of which they can be proud.

○ Repeat and clarify key words the teacher has said.

○ Provide feedback at the end of each session to remind the pupil what has been achieved. For example, 'You did really well today, Abdul. You wrote six sentences with not one spelling mistake. I'm proud of you.'

○ Support the pupil in physical education to ensure they are able to achieve some of the tasks set for other pupils. A helping hand to assist the pupil with handstands and the use of a large ball in catching and throwing activities are examples.

○ Ensure the pupil has all the necessary resources at the beginning of each lesson.

○ Keep records of the child's progress to assist the teacher with weekly planning and differentiation.

## Additional help

○ Educational psychologists (see page 26).

○ Specialist teachers (see page 26).

○ Occupational therapists may assess, suggest exercise programmes to assist with the development of fine and gross motor skills, recommend equipment or modifications if appropriate, and recommend alterations to the environment.

○ Physiotherapists may assist with programmes of exercise, which can be carried out by TAs and parents.

○ Speech and language therapists may provide a remedial programme if there is a speech difficulty.

○ A paediatrician may be involved in a multi-agency diagnosis.

○ Parents (see page 26).

## Useful addresses and websites

Dyspraxia Foundation
8 West Alley, Hitchin,
Hertfordshire SG5 1EG
Tel.: 01462 454986
Fax.: 01462 455052
*www.dyspraxiafoundation.org.uk*

British Association/College of
Occupational Therapists
106–114 Borough High Street,
Southwark, London SE1 1LB
*www.cot.org.uk*

## Useful books

*How to Understand and Support Children with Dyspraxia*, Lois Addy. LDA, 2003

*Dyspraxia: A guide for teachers and parents* (Resource Materials for Teachers), Kate Ripley, Bob Daines and Jenny Barratt. David Fulton, 1997

*Dyspraxia in the Early Years: Identifying and supporting children with movement difficulties*, Christine Macintyre. David Fulton, 2000

*Understanding Developmental Dyspraxia: A textbook for students and professionals*, Madeleine Portwood. David Fulton, 2000

## Useful resources

*Write from the Start, Speed Up!, Writestart Desktop*
LDA

# Behavioural, emotional and social difficulties

This area identified in the Code of Practice relates to pupils with problems with their behaviour and/or emotional and social development. These pupils demonstrate a wide variety of symptoms ranging from withdrawn and isolated behaviour to disruptive hyperactivity. This is the area that often creates the most difficulty for the teacher and is one in which the TA may be particularly usefully deployed.

A DfEE circular (DfEE 1994b) identifies the types of behaviour that characterise emotional and behavioural difficulties:

- Personal level: through low self-image, anxiety, depression or withdrawal, or through resentment, vindictiveness or defiance.
- Verbal level: the child may be silent or threaten or swear a great deal.
- Non-verbal level: clinging, truancy, failure to observe rules, disruptiveness, destructiveness, aggression or violence.
- Work/skills level: an inability or unwillingness to work without direct supervision, to concentrate in order to complete tasks, or to follow instructions.

## Strategies for teachers

- Establish regular telephone contact with parents to inform them of success and achievement as well as of problem behaviour.
- Provide pupils with a behaviour target sheet and discuss it at the end of each day. The target may have been to complete a specified piece of work in a given time, or to put their hand up before answering questions instead of shouting out.

Andy Vass recommends the following ten top tips (Vass 2002):
- Focus on the positive – catch them being good.
- Intentional ignoring – ignore minor misdemeanours.
- Positive cueing – thank the pupil who is on task and clarify the behaviour that pleases you.
- Use positive directions – say what behaviour you want, not what you don't want.
- Rule reminders – keep clarifying what the rule is for a pupil who keeps on breaking it, and why it is important to keep the rule. For example, if you run down the corridor you are likely to hurt someone.
- Refocusing with questions – ask casual questions to refocus the pupil instead of making too much of the inappropriate behaviour.
- 'When . . . then' – establishes the promise of a reward in exchange for a task that is completed: 'Kurdip, when you have finished your maths, and you have ten sums to complete, then you may go on the computer.'
- Acknowledge and redirect – 'I understand you want to talk to your friends and I want you to . . . '

- Either/or language – use language of choice. 'You can choose to work quietly or you can choose to stay behind.' It is important to provide choice since you are inviting the pupil to take on the responsibility that accompanies the decision.
- Follow through with an agreed consequence – if you have named a consequence for poor behaviour, you must stick to it.

## How teaching assistants can help

- Administer the checklist as a means of providing evidence (see page 60).
- Spend time with the pupils to work on issues regarding self-esteem and building relationships.
- Sit near pupils likely to offend and act as a second pair of eyes.
- Observe the class while the teacher is talking and take down the names of pupils not sticking to the rules to save the teacher having to interrupt the general flow of the lesson.
- Remove from the classroom pupils who need time to cool down. Accompany them on a walk around the playground or take them to a quiet room. Some schools have a designated sanctuary set up especially for the purpose.
- Seek help from outside the classroom if a pupil refuses to leave, and constitutes a danger within the classroom. In some schools a pupil is handed a red card by the teacher or TA to take it to a designated person – usually a member of the senior management team. TAs working on their own with a group away from the class should have a means of seeking help, by issuing a red card or following a different system advocated by their school.
- Assist with dining-hall duties to ensure the pupil is aware of acceptable table manners.
- Keep records noting incidences of dysfunctional behaviour.

## Additional help

- Educational psychologists (see page 26).
- Specialist teachers (see page 26).
- Parents (see page 26).
- Counsellors may be involved in providing a confidential service and listening ear for the pupil, offering suggestions about how they may be able to deal with their problem in a way that is acceptable.
- Child psychiatrists may be involved if behavioural problems exhibited by the child suggest some deep-rooted problems; examples are excessive violence and strange behaviour.
- Bereavement counsellors (if appropriate).

## Useful books

*Improving Behaviour and Raising Self-esteem in the Classroom*, Giles Barrow, Emma Bradshaw and Trudi Newton. David Fulton, 2001

"Some schools have a designated sanctuary."

**Useful address and website**

ADDISS
(National Attention Deficit Disorder Information and Support Service)
PO Box 340
Edgware
Middlesex
HA8 9HL
Tel.: 0208 952 2800
*www.addiss.co.uk*

*Making Sense of Behaviour,* Rob Long. NASEN, 2000

*How to Teach and Manage Children with ADHD,* Fintan O'Regan. LDA, 2002

# Sensory and/or physical needs

Some pupils with physical and sensory needs have no problems within school – they do not have an SEN. However, for some pupils their condition will have an impact on their access to the National Curriculum, and as a result they may need extra support. The Code of Practice 2001 explains this as follows:

> There is a wide spectrum of sensory, multi-sensory and physical difficulties. The sensory range extends from profound and permanent deafness or visual impairment throught to lesser levels of loss, which may only be temporary. Physical impairments may arise from physical, neurological or metabolic causes that only require appropriate access to educational facilities and equipment; others may lead to more complex and social needs; a few children will have multi-sensory difficulties some with associated physical difficulties. (Para. 7:62)

## *Pupils with hearing impairment*

Hearing loss experienced by a pupil will be conductive or permanent. Conductive hearing loss is intermittent, and may be due to excessive ear wax, a heavy cold or a respiratory infection, which causes fluid to build up in the middle ear. Pupils with permanent hearing problems may be experiencing anything from a profound loss to a mild one. The impairment may be deteriorating, fluctuating or stable. Most pupils with profound hearing loss will have been identified before school age is reached and hopefully will be benefiting from the provision of appropriate resources to aid hearing. However, some pupils' difficulties may develop at a later stage and we need to watch out for the warning signs, many of which can be found in the checklist (page 61).

## Strategies for teachers

- Make sure that the room is bright enough for the child to see clearly any visual cues or posters, boards, charts and so on that are on view.
- Do not accentuate speech or speak more slowly – most children will lip read well as long as you maintain a normal pace and your speech is clear.
- Make sure that the child is looking at the teacher or TA before instructions are given.
- Do not talk when your back is turned to the child (for instance to write on the board). Make sure your face is visible at all times.
- Try to avoid a noisy classroom – ensure that children speak one at a time during discussion or question-and-answer time.
- Use gestures to aid understanding.

**Useful addresses and websites**

British Deaf Association
1–3 Worship Street, London EC2A 2AB
Tel.: 020 758 83520
*www.britishdeafassociation.org.uk*

National Deaf Children's Society
15 Dufferin Street, London EC1Y 8UR
Tel.: 020 7490 8656
*www.ndcs.org.uk*

◐ Do not interrupt a conversation to correct a child's speech.

◐ Allow the pupil to turn off their hearing aid when conditions around are particularly noisy.

### How teaching assistants can help pupils

◐ Administer the checklist as a means of gathering evidence (see page 61).

◐ Keep records of the child's progress to assist the teacher with weekly planning and differentiation.

◐ Sit next to the pupil in order to clarify certain points or repeat crucial words to ensure they understand the points made.

◐ Stay in close proximity to a child outside or in physical education when they need to hear verbal instructions.

◐ Encourage the pupil to make verbal contributions to the lesson by prompting. 'Hayley, you know the answer to this. Go on, have a go!'

◐ Escort the pupil from the classroom if they become distressed or disruptive.

◐ Check that equipment such as a hearing aid is working.

◐ Carry out any particular programmes of work recommended by the professional who is monitoring the progress of the child.

### Additional help

◐ Educational psychologists (see page 26).

◐ Speech and language therapists may provide a remedial programme.

◐ A paediatrician may be involved in a multi-agency diagnosis.

◐ Specialist teachers (see page 26).

◐ Parents (see page 26).

◐ The audiologist at the local hospital who will take responsibility for diagnosis and recommending appropriate treatment.

### Useful books

*Deaf and Hearing Impaired Pupils in Mainstream Schools,* Linda Watson, Susan Gregory and Stephen Powers. David Fulton, 1999

*Deaf Children, their Families and Professionals: Dismantling barriers (quality in secondary schools and colleges),* Sarah Beazley and Michael Moore. David Fulton, 1995

*Hearing Impairment* (Spotlight on Special Educational Needs), Linda Watson. NASEN, 1996

## Pupils with visual impairment

Pupils with visual impairment may experience difficulties in different ways. A pupil has a visual impairment if their vision cannot be corrected to normal by using some means of optical correction. The pupil may have difficulty with scanning or with visual fixation. They may have problems in maintaining

*Frequently, deaf children enter school lacking the communication skills to understand the efforts of those attempting to prepare them verbally for the experience and what is more, lacking the ability to communicate their subsequent bewilderment.*

*From* Being Deaf: The experience of deafness, *ed. George Taylor and Juliet Bishop (Open University, 1990)*

and changing focus both at long and short distances; or what they see may be grossly distorted. Their visual field may be restricted, they may suffer from visual fatigue, or they may have a problem in recognising different colours.

## Strategies for teachers

- Use a sloping desk.
- Use additional lighting to help, for example an anglepoise lamp.
- A laptop computer with a facility for enlarged print may be useful.
- The use of specialised software such as textHELP, with a voice that accompanies the text on the screen, may help.
- Encourage the use of thick black felt-tip pens and wide-lined paper.
- Make use of a hand-held tape recorder for taking notes and doing homework.
- Check on the position of the pupil in the classroom.
- Explore the use of coloured paper.
- Check whether the child needs help when walking around the school.
- Allow more time for the completion of work.
- Ensure the pupil participates fully in school life, making certain that they have a friend at break times.
- Use brightly coloured balls and games equipment to help participation in physical education and games.

## How teaching assistants can help

- Administer the checklist as a means of gathering evidence (see page 62).
- Teach word-processing skills.
- Assist with the organisation and checking of equipment, for example Braille resources, computers and magnifying glasses.
- Differentiate visual resources so they are accessible to the pupil. For example photocopy worksheets and books, enlarging the font.
- Teach self-help skills such as eating, dressing and personal grooming.
- Ensure the classroom is tidy to prevent the pupil bumping into unfamiliar objects.

## Additional support

- Educational psychologists (see page 26).
- Specialist teachers (see page 26).
- School medical officer, who will be involved as part of a multi-professional diagnosis.
- Parents (see page 26).

### Useful addresses and websites

Royal National Institute for the Blind (RNIB)
105 Judd Street, London WC1H 9NE
Tel.: 020 7388 1266
*www.rnib.org.uk*

Partially Sighted Society
Queens Road, Doncaster DN1 2NX
Tel.: 01302 323132

National Blind Children Society (NBCS)
Bradbury House, Market Street,
Highbridge, Somerset TA9 3BW
Tel.: 01278 764764
*www.nbcs.org.uk*

National Library for the Blind
Far Cromwell Road, Bredbury,
Stockport SK6 2SG
Tel.: 0161 355 2000
*www.nlb-online.org*

LEEDS COLLEGE OF BUILDING
LIBRARY

## Useful books

*Visual Impairment: Access to education for children and young people,* edited by Heather Mason and Stephen McCall, with Christine Arter, Mike McLinden and Juliet Stone. David Fulton, 1997

*Children with Visual Impairment in Mainstream Settings,* Christine Arter, Heather Mason, Stephen McCall, Mike McLinden and Juliet Stone in association with the School of Education, University of Birmingham. David Fulton, 1999

*Learning through Touch: Supporting children with visual impairment and additional difficulties,* Mike McLinden and Stephen McCall. David Fulton, 2002

# Medical conditions

The SEN Code of Practice also identifies the fact that some pupils in schools have a medical condition. However most of these pupils will not have an SEN but they should be included in a school register of pupils with medical conditions. The following information may be helpful in raising awareness of implications of particular conditions and providing ways to offer support for pupils. Although the response has been written in reference to the TA, it can, of course apply to any willing staff member.

## *Anaphylaxis*

Children with this condition will experience an extreme allergic reaction to a particular source. This may be related to a food such as nuts or dairy products; insect stings and latex may also be responsible. The pupil may experience difficulty with swallowing or breathing, or feel nauseous and have stomach cramps and swelling of the face. They may collapse and become unconscious.

### Teaching assistant response

A member of staff needs to be willing to take on the responsibility for administering an injection of adrenaline. This should follow training from a medically trained professional. The injection should be administered as soon as the reaction is suspected and an ambulance called. If there is no improvement, a second injection can be administered after 5 to 10 minutes, as directed. The TA should be aware of the source of allergy and prevent the child coming into contact with it. They may decide, for example, to escort a pupil quietly from a classroom where there is a persistent bee, if they have an allergy to its sting.

### Useful book

*Life Threatening Allergic Reactions: Understanding and coping with anaphylaxis,* Deryk Williams *et al.* Piatkus Books, 1997

**Useful address and website**

Anaphylaxis Campaign
PO Box 275,
Farnborough GU14 6SX
Tel.: 01252 546100
Helpline: 01252 542029
*www.anaphylaxis.org.uk*

**Useful address and website**

Asthma UK
Summit House, 70 Wilson Street,
London EC2A 2DB
Tel.: 020 7786 4900
Helpline: 08457 01 02 03
*www.asthma.org.uk*

## Asthma

Pupils with asthma experience a narrowing of their airways and will become breathless and wheezy when they have a cold or when they come into contact with certain stimuli or triggers. These will vary, but the most common are grass pollen, house dust, animal fur and cold air. Physical activity and stress may also trigger an attack.

### Teaching assistant response

Many pupils will have been provided with inhalers. Reliever inhalers, which are usually blue, relax the muscles surrounding the narrow airways. Children may also need a preventer inhaler, which is usually brown, red or orange. This helps to control swelling and inflammation and is used every day even if the child feels well. All inhalers should be named and left in a safe yet accessible place. The TA could be responsible for escorting the pupils from the classroom and overseeing the administration of the inhaler, following appropriate training. If the symptoms persist, an ambulance must be called for.

### Useful books

*Caring for Children with Asthma* (What You Really Need to Know about . . .), Jan Hurst. Marshall Editions, 1999

*Asthma Sourcebook,* edited by Annemarie Muth. Omnigraphics, US, 2000

**Useful addresses and websites**

SCOPE
6 Market Road,
London N7 9PW
Tel.: 0808 800 3333
*www.scope.org.uk*

Foundation for Conductive Education
Cannon Hill House, Russell Road,
Moseley, Birmingham B13 8RD
Tel.: 0121 449 1569
*www.conductive-education.org.uk*

## Cerebral palsy

Children with cerebral palsy will not all manifest the same symptoms; these will depend on the severity of the condition. They may have difficulty in walking, or their speech may be affected. Some who have this condition produce involuntary movements and some have problems with visual perception. Certain pupils will manage perfectly well in mainstream schools and need only to be placed on a medical register. Others will need TA support, and some will require a place in a special school.

### Teaching assistant response

The TA may be involved by assisting the pupil in moving around school, monitoring at playtimes, helping with dressing for swimming and physical education, helping with physical activities and so on.

### Useful book

*Children with Cerebral Palsy,* Elaine Geralis. Woodbine House, 1998

**Useful address and website**

Cystic Fibrosis Trust
11 London Road, Bromley,
Kent BR1 1BY
Tel.: 020 8464 7211
*www.cftrust.org.uk*

## Cystic fibrosis

Cystic fibrosis is a genetic disease. Sufferers have a disturbance in the mucus-secreting glands, which leads to the clogging of some organs, especially the lungs and pancreas, with thick sticky mucus. Children with cystic fibrosis will usually experience a persistent cough and may have a lot of time away from

*Victoria: I'm always hungry at break time. My friends and I always have a snack before we do anything else.*

*From* I Have Cystic Fibrosis, *Brenda Pettenuzzo (Franklin Watts, 1998)*

**Useful address and website**

Diabetes UK
Macleod House, 10 Parkway,
London NW1 7AA
Tel.: 020 7424 1000
*www.diabetes.org.uk*

**Useful address and website**

Down's Syndrome Association
Langdon Down Centre,
2a Langdon Park,
Teddington TW11 9PS
Tel.: 0845 230 0372
*www.downs-syndrome.org.uk*

school through hospitalisation with chest infections. It is important for them to eat as often as possible as they do not fully absorb their food.

## Teaching assistant response

Refer to parental and medical advice. Monitor the behaviour of the child closely.

## Useful book

*Cystic Fibrosis – Overcoming common problems,* Jane Chumbley. Sheldon Press, 1999

## Diabetes

Diabetic pupils do not have the ability to control their blood sugar levels, which must be checked regularly so they are neither too high (hyperglycaemia), or low (hypoglycaemia or hypo). Most children will have Type 1 diabetes meaning they no longer produce insulin and have to inject themselves, usually twice a day. Pupils must be allowed to eat regularly during the day since lack of food or strenuous exercise may cause a hypo. Symptoms of an impending attack include drowsiness, sweating, shaking and glazed eyes. Hyperglycaemia may be the result of missed insulin, eating a lot of starchy food or being unwell. The child is likely to be thirsty, tired and have headaches.

## Response

If the child has a hypo, the TA needs to provide glucose tablets or sugary food or drink immediately, and must ensure that these are always available in school. If pupils do not rapidly recover, an ambulance should be called for. In hyperglycaemia, the child will need to drink water or sugar-free drinks and parents must be contacted.

## Useful book

*Insulin Dependent Diabetes in Children, Adolescents and Adults,* Ragar Hanas. Class Publishing, 2003

## Down's Syndrome

An extra chromosome in each body cell causes this syndrome. Physical characteristics include an enlarged tongue and an upward slant to the eyes. Down's Syndrome children are particularly prone to infections and viruses such as colds. The syndrome is associated with difficulties in learning, but in fact some pupils achieve reasonable academic standards in school.

## Teaching assistant response

Some children with this syndrome present no problem in an ordinary classroom, and will need no extra support. However, most have learning difficulties and will require help. Often the problems will relate to delayed fine and gross motor skills, short concentration span, significant speech and language delay and a weak auditory learning style.

## Useful books
*Children with Down's Syndrome: A guide for teachers and teaching assistants in mainstream primary and secondary schools* (Resource Materials for Teachers), Stephanie Lorenz. David Fulton, 1998

*Gross Motor Skills in Children with Down's Syndrome*, Patricia Winders. Woodbine House, 1992

## Eczema
Pupils with eczema suffer from itchy dry skin which, if scratched, may bleed and become infected. There are various types, the most common being atopic, often associated with hayfever and asthma. In severe cases pupils will need to have a prescribed cream administered at school. Certain factors may make the eczema worse, including wool, soaps, pollen, sweating and stress.

### Teaching assistant response
The TA should be aware of pupils with this condition. They should attempt to distract a pupil who is scratching the skin. They may also apply emollient cream to the affected areas in accordance with parental and medical instruction.

### Useful books
*Kim has Eczema*, Andrew Pattison. Hyland House Publishing, 1998

*Eczema and contact dermatitis* (Fast Facts), John Berth-Jones *et al.* Health Press, 2003

## Epilepsy
Epilepsy is a transitory disturbance of the brain which begins and ceases spontaneously. These uncontrolled electrical impulses usually result from a damaged or abnormal area of brain tissue. Seizures are divided into two types, referred to as generalised and partial. Generalised seizures involve both hemispheres and are accompanied by a loss of consciousness. In partial seizures a specific part of the brain is involved and the nature of the seizures may be simple or complex.

Episodes usually do not last long, but they may occur very frequently. The condition is usually controlled by drugs, but these have side-effects which impact on the ability to concentrate and remain focused.

### Teaching assistant response
Some children are able to let you know that they are about to have a seizure as they have an aura or premonition. When symptoms of an imminent attack

---

**Useful address and website**
National Eczema Society
Hill House, Highgate Hill,
London N19 5NA
Tel.: 020 7281 3553
*www.eczema.org*

*Salvatore's fits are caused by several things. If the light is bright and it shines in his eyes he may have a fit or he may just begin to flick his hand across his forehead.*

*Salvatore: I used to sit near the window, but my teacher noticed the sun was in my eyes and changed my place.*

*From* I Have Epilepsy, *Brenda Pettenuzzo (Franklin Watts, 1989)*

**Useful addresses and websites**

National Society for Epilepsy
Chesham Lane, Chalfont St Peter,
Buckinghamshire SL9 0RJ
Tel.: 01494 601300
*www.epilepsynse.org.uk*

Epilepsy Action
New Anstey House, Gate Way Drive,
Yeadon, Leeds LS19 7XY
Tel.: 0113 210 8800
Helpline: 0808 800 5050
*www.epilepsy.org.uk*

appear the TA must ensure the child is in a place where they will not suffer physical injury. If convulsions do occur, the child should not be moved unless they are in a dangerous place, and the area around should be cleared. They could administer first aid after consultation with parents and after training if necessary. Medical emergencies are rare in epilepsy but in the event of a seizure continuing, an ambulance should be called. The TA could also help with the administration of drugs if the child has to take them during the day.

### Useful books
*Epilepsy: A practical guide* (Resource Materials for Teachers), Mike Johnson and Gill Parkinson. David Fulton, 2002

*Epilepsy* (The Facts) (2nd edition), Anthony Hopkins and Richard Appleton. Paperbacks, 1996

## Glue ear
Glue ear affects many primary school children. It is important to be aware of the situation since it causes a fluctuating hearing loss. It would be wise to ensure that the pupil's parents inform you when their child has a problem so that necessary steps can be taken. Glue ear is usually temporary and is the result of build up of a mucus-like fluid in the middle ear. There is concern that during the critical stages of development it may cause longer-term speech and language problems and it may also affect behaviour.

**Useful address and website**

Royal National Institute for deaf and
hard of hearing people (RNID)
19–23 Featherstone Street,
London EC1Y 8SL
Tel.: 020 7296 8000
Helpline: 0808 808 0123
*www.rnid.org.uk*

### Teaching assistant response
The TA should support the pupil in the same way as recommended for pupils with hearing impairments (see page 41), when the problem arises. They must be aware of and watch out for the tell-tale signs – lack of attention in class, speaking loudly and failure to hear instructions – and then take appropriate action.

### Useful book
*Glue Ear in Childhood*, Richard Maw. MacKeith Press, 1995

## Haemophilia
Haemophilia is a hereditary disorder of the blood which interferes with its clotting. It usually affects males. The haemophiliac is liable to have repeated episodes of bleeding. Bouts may be bought on by falls, blows and exercise, and some appear to occur spontaneously. Bleeding occasionally occurs in the joints, which may cause severe pain and eventual damage.

**Useful address and website**

Haemophilia Society
First Floor, Petersham House,
57a Hatton Garden, London EC1N 8JG
Tel.: 020 7831 1020
Helpline: 0800 018 6068
*www.haemophilia.org.uk*

### Teaching assistant response
When a pupil is cut or scratched there is usually no cause for concern; a sticking plaster should suffice (check whether the child is allergic to them first). In the case of a severe attack of bleeding, parents should be immediately informed or

the child should be taken to hospital so that an injection of the clotting factor can be administered. In the absence of the parent, the TA could accompany the child.

### Useful books
*Understanding Haemophilia,* Marie Berger. Ashgrove Press, 1989

*Haemophilia in the Child and Adult,* Margaret Hilgartner. Masson Publications, 1983

## Heart conditions
Most children with heart problems will have either experienced them since birth or acquired them as a result of rheumatic fever. Some of these pupils will need an operation at some stage, and it is important to follow the advice of the consultant closely regarding the provision that needs to be made in school. These children may not be able to take part in contact sports or play in the playground. However, on the whole, they need little extra attention, although they may become breathless at times and need to rest.

### Teaching assistant response
This will largely depend on the information provided by parents and doctors.

### Useful books
*Heart Conditions,* Sara Lewis. Abacus, 1994

*Heart Conditions*, Elizabeth Walker. Penguin Books, 1994

## HIV/Aids
The child with HIV/Aids may be seen as a threat because of the possibility of spreading the condition. It is particularly important that the child's situation is treated with the strictest confidentiality; otherwise they may be in danger of becoming a social outcast. HIV can only be transmitted through the blood. If the child bleeds heavily steps should be taken to prevent transmission.

### Teaching assistant response
The TA should wear disposable gloves when attending to the child, and should make sure that any abrasions they have are suitably covered. The child is likely to have to take medication during the school day and the TA may be involved in this. The school policy will provide further information regarding provision for HIV pupils.

### Useful books
*HIV and AIDs, Testing, screening and confidentiality (Issues in biomedical ethics),* edited by Rebecca Bennet and Charles Erin. Clarendon Press, 2001

**Useful address and website**

British Heart Foundation
14 Fitzhardinge Street,
London W1H 6DH
Tel.: 020 7935 0185
*www.bhf.org.uk*

**Useful address and website**

Terence Higgins Trust
314–320 Gray's Inn Road,
London WC1X 8DP
Tel.: 020 7812 1600
*www.tht.org.uk*

*... just over a year ago, Tony decided his disability was holding him back and he asked to move to another more suitable school.*

*Tony: My school is called the 'Elizabeth Fry School', and I've been going there for a year now. I used to go to the same school as my sisters.*

*From* I Have Muscular Dystrophy, *by Brenda Pettenuzzo (Franklin Watts, 1989)*

**Useful address and website**
Muscular Dystrophy Campaign
7–11 Prescott Place, London SW4 6BS
Tel.: 020 7720 8055
*www.muscular-dystrophy.org*

**Useful address and website**
Prader-Willi Syndrome Association
(PWSA) (UK)
125a London Road, Derby DE1 2QQ
Tel.: 01332 365676
*www.pwsa.co.uk*

*The End of Innocence: Britain in the time of AIDs,* Simon Garfield. Faber and Faber, 1995

## Muscular dystrophy

Muscular dystrophy is an inherited disease involving deterioration and wasting of the voluntary muscles. Some pupils will be severely affected while others will experience comparatively mild symptoms. Those with the severe form will lose their ability to walk and the muscles in the hand and arm may be affected, causing problems with writing and drawing. Children with muscular dystrophy tend also to have a learning difficulty and emotional problems are common.

### Teaching assistant response
The teaching assistant may be employed to assist the pupil in school. If the pupil is still mobile, the assistance may be needed to help them negotiate the busy parts of the school. The TA must learn to use the various special resources available, such as special computer programmes and keyboards.

### Useful books
*Muscular Dystrophy in Children: A guide for families,* Irwin Siegal. Demos Medical Publishing Inc., 1999

*Muscular Dystrophy* (The Facts), Alan Emery. Oxford University Press, 2000

## Prader-Willi Syndrome

Prader-Willi Syndrome (PWS) is caused by an abnormality on chromosome 15. The main symptoms are poor muscle tone, overeating, speech and language problems, emotional immaturity and behavioural problems. Physical characteristics often include small hands and feet and almond-shaped eyes, and those affected may have fairer hair and eye colouring than other family members. Most children with PWS will have moderate learning difficulties. Usually, reading and writing skills develop well but ability in maths and abstract thinking may cause educational difficulties. Short-term auditory memory is weak but long-term memory is often a strength.

### Teaching assistant response
Deal with behaviour according to previously agreed guidelines. Ensure the pupil is not left alone with food, and encourage social skills such as turn-taking and not interrupting. Encouraging pupils to exercise would be beneficial as this helps pupils to control their weight and improves muscle tone.

### Useful book
*Prader-Willi Syndrome: A practical guide* (Resource Materials for Teachers), Jackie Waters. David Fulton, 1999

**Useful address and website**

Tourette Syndrome (UK) Association
Southbank House, Black Prince Road,
London SW1 7SJ
Tel.: 0207 793 2357
Helpline: 0845 458 1252
*www.tsa.org.uk*

## Tourette Syndrome

Tourette Syndrome is an inherited neurological disorder in which the body develops motor and vocal tics, usually apparent by the time a child reaches the age of 15. The severity will vary from day to day. Some children are able to control their tics at times, but they will often reappear at a later date. The most common motor tics include eye blinking or rolling, nose twitching, lip smacking and shoulder shrugging; while vocal tics include throat clearing, swearing, stammering and shouting.

### Teaching assistant response

Pupils will need help with their organisational skills and behaviour. Their tics should in general be ignored, but when they become severe or distressing it may be appropriate to escort the pupil out of the class so they have some privacy. The pupil should be seated near a door so they have an easy way out when they need to leave. Pay attention to positive behaviour and find a reward that is satisfying for the pupil. Check regularly with the pupil to ensure they are not being bullied.

### Useful book

*Tourette Syndrome: A practical guide for teachers, parents and carers*, Amber Carroll and Mary Robertson. David Fulton, 2000

## Williams Syndrome

Williams Syndrome is a rare genetic disorder which gives rise to both physical and mental disabilities. The condition can only be diagnosed with a blood test and often goes unrecognised for many years. Pupils with Williams Syndrome may be small for their age, have low-pitched voices and be overfriendly, yet they may be overanxious and fearful. They have very sensitive hearing and may display obsessive behaviour. They will have poor communication skills and will usually have a learning difficulty ranging from mild to severe. Other problems they may suffer from are heart conditions, infantile hypercalcaemia, dental problems and raised blood pressure. Children affected may experience feeding and sleeping difficulties and have toilet problems.

**Useful address and website**

Williams Syndrome Foundation (UK)
161 High Street, Tonbridge,
Kent TN9 1BX
Tel.: 01732 365152
*www.williams-syndrome.org.uk*

### Teaching assistant response

Pupils with Williams Syndrome often have a poor attention span and work best in a distraction-free environment. They would benefit from some 1:1 attention. They need firm and consistent handling, and may benefit from a reward system which encourages them to complete work in a certain period of time. Be aware that the pupil may need to visit the toilet regularly.

### Useful publications

The following are available from the Williams Syndrome Foundation.

*Williams Syndrome Explained* (information leaflet)
*Guidelines for Teachers*
Video: *Williams Syndrome: Williams's People*

## Support for parents

Most of the organisations referred to in this section will have arranged local support groups for parents. The information here has been provided by Contact a Family (CAF), a UK charity that helps families who care for children with any disability or special need. They are also a major source of information about rare disorders and are able to assist affected adults as well as children.

The CAF Directory Online contains details of many medical conditions and also information about patient support groups. They may be able to provide information about medical conditions not listed here.

The helpline (0808 808 3555) can provide information for parents, carers and professionals on:

- parent support groups;
- specific conditions;
- local services;
- a wide range of topics, such as benefits, siblings and holidays.

## Final thoughts

So there we have it. I hope this book has provided you with some useful ideas, food for thought and additional knowledge. I think the challenge of educating pupils in mainstream schools is an exciting and hugely worthwhile one to meet.

We must, however, accept that we will not be able to get it right all the time for all pupils. It will not always be possible or desirable to maintain all pupils within mainstream schools despite the excellent services offered by teachers, TAs and LEAs. There will always, in my opinion, be an important place for special schools. There are many excellent special schools in existence that have a wealth of expertise and care. They are the appropriate places to meet the needs of certain pupils who will thrive in a special setting and would not fit well into the confines of a mainstream school. There is a place for all of us.

I hope you found this book useful. Thank you for reading it.

Final food for thought

From 'You are a marvel'

And what do we teach our children? We teach them that two and two make four, and that Paris is the capital of France.
When will we also teach them what they are?
We should say to each of them: Do you know what you are? You are a marvel. You are unique. In all the years that have passed, there has never been another child like you. Your legs, your arms, your clever fingers, the way you move. You may become a Shakespeare, a Michelangelo, a Beethoven. You have the capacity for anything. Yes, you are a marvel.

*By Pablo Casals, in* Chicken Soup for the Soul, *edited by Jack Canfield and Mark Hansen (Vermilion, 2000)*

# Appendix

*Checklists*

# Speech and language difficulties

## Checklist

Name:                                          Observer:

| | | Yes | No |
|---|---|---|---|
| 1. | Has difficulty with the production of speech and functions at a level below that of the peer group. | | |
| 2. | Has a problem finding words and being able to put them together in order to produce language others can understand. | | |
| 3. | Has difficulty participating in group discussions and question-and-answer sessions. | | |
| 4. | Becomes frustrated or upset at their lack of ability to communicate, with consequent behavioural difficulties. | | |
| 5. | Fails to respond appropriately to the verbal input of others, so often has difficulty building relationships with other children. | | |
| 6. | Unable to express thoughts and feelings adequately, so needs often go unmet. | | |
| 7. | Has trouble in communicating through speech, with a consequent impact on literacy skills; may be able to make progress in other areas of the curriculum which are not dependent on language. | | |
| 8. | May be thought to be ill-mannered because of inability to use appropriate social language. | | |

Other observations you wish to make.

Date:

© *How to support and teach children with special educational needs* LDA                    Permission to Photocopy

# Autism/Asperger Syndrome

## Checklist

Name:                                        Observer:

| | | Yes | No |
|---|---|---|---|
| 1. | Has difficulty with social relationships: wants to be involved socially but has difficulty in understanding non-verbal signals. | | |
| 2. | Experiences problems with communication: may speak fluently, but is unable to engage with the reactions of people and may talk on despite the fact the other person has clearly lost interest in the conversation. | | |
| 3. | Has good language skills, but sounds overprecise or overliteral. 'You must pull your socks up' will be taken literally. | | |
| 4. | Lacks imagination: often very skilled at learning facts and figures, but finds it hard to think in abstract ways. | | |
| 5. | Develops an almost obsessive special hobby or interest, which will often involve arranging or memorising facts such as train timetables or historical events. | | |
| 6. | Loves routine: will often find change upsetting, such as an alteration in the timetable or travelling to school using a different route. | | |
| 7. | Unaware of social conventions and will appear ill-mannered: may interrupt lessons, or go to the front of queues. | | |
| 8. | Appears clumsy and ill-coordinated. | | |
| 9. | Is oversensitive to light and sound. | | |
| 10. | Is insensitive to low level of pain. | | |

Other observations you wish to make.




Date:

# General learning difficulties

## Checklist

Name:                                    Observer:

|     |                                                                                                    | Yes | No |
|-----|----------------------------------------------------------------------------------------------------|-----|----|
| 1.  | Has failed to reach the desired age-appropriate performance within the National Curriculum.        |     |    |
| 2.  | Is unable to achieve the level of work expected from the objectives set within literacy and numeracy frameworks. |     |    |
| 3.  | Attainment in literacy and numeracy interferes with access to the rest of the curriculum.          |     |    |
| 4.  | Assessments for cognitive ability, which may have been carried out by the school, result in a low score. |     |    |
| 5.  | Fails to reach set targets felt to be appropriate.                                                 |     |    |
| 6.  | Quality and presentation of the pupil's work fails to reflect the general standard of the class.   |     |    |
| 7.  | Displays confusion in areas that most of the peer group understand.                                |     |    |
| 8.  | Needs extra time to complete work.                                                                 |     |    |

Other observations you wish to make.



Date:

# Dyslexia

## Checklist

Name:                                    Observer:

| | | Yes | No |
|---|---|---|---|
| 1. | Displays average or above-average profile of abilities and attainments in non-literacy-related areas and scores well on assessments not related to areas of literacy. | | |
| 2. | Has good general knowledge and oral ability. | | |
| 3. | Demonstrates mismatch between spoken and written responses. | | |
| 4. | Has problems with number/letter formation. | | |
| 5. | Often reverses words when reading or spelling (e.g. bat/tab). | | |
| 6. | Has problems sequencing letters appropriately when spelling. | | |
| 7. | Shows a tendency to miss out letters regularly in words, or words when writing sentences. | | |
| 8. | Takes longer than peers to complete written work. | | |
| 9. | Experiences problems with discrimination between similar sounds. | | |
| 10. | Has difficulty in matching correct sounds in reading. | | |
| 11. | Has problems with general organisation. | | |
| 12. | Has a difficulty with rote learning times tables, months of the year, the alphabet. | | |

Other observations you wish to make.

Date:

© How to support and teach children with special educational needs LDA

Permission to Photocopy

# Dyspraxia

## Checklist (as advised by the Dyspraxia Foundation)

Name:                                           Observer:

|     |                                                                                                          | Yes | No |
|-----|----------------------------------------------------------------------------------------------------------|-----|----|
| 1.  | Has problems in adapting to the structured school routine.                                               |     |    |
| 2.  | Experiences difficulties with physical education: may not be able to accomplish or attempt some physical tasks. |     |    |
| 3.  | Is slow at dressing and is unable to tie shoelaces.                                                      |     |    |
| 4.  | Produces barely legible handwriting; immature drawing and copying skills.                               |     |    |
| 5.  | Capable of only limited concentration; poor listening skills.                                           |     |    |
| 6.  | Literal use of language: believes you if you say ' I saw red!' and may respond, 'I can't see any red.'  |     |    |
| 7.  | Demonstrates an inability to remember more than two to three instructions.                              |     |    |
| 8.  | Is often slow to complete classwork.                                                                    |     |    |
| 9.  | Has high levels of motor activity/restlessness; fidgets.                                                |     |    |
| 10. | Often flaps hands or claps when excited.                                                                |     |    |
| 11. | Has a tendency to become easily distressed and emotional.                                               |     |    |
| 12. | Has a problem in co-ordinating a knife and fork.                                                        |     |    |
| 13. | Lacks the ability to form relationships with other children.                                            |     |    |
| 14. | Often experiences sleeping difficulties, including wakefulness at night and nightmares.                 |     |    |
| 15. | Reports physical symptoms such as migraine, headaches or feeling sick.                                  |     |    |

Other observations you wish to make.

Date:

© How to support and teach children with special educational needs LDA          Permission to Photocopy

# Behavioural/emotional/social difficulties

## Checklist

Name:                                          Observer:

| | | Yes | No |
|---|---|---|---|
| 1. | Demonstrates a limited concentration span. | | |
| 2. | Often talks out of turn. | | |
| 3. | Leaves seat without permission. | | |
| 4. | Persistently breaks the school rules (e.g. chewing in class, not wearing the school uniform). | | |
| 5. | Frequently deliberately disturbs other pupils. | | |
| 6. | Leaves the class without permission. | | |
| 7. | Often shouts out in class. | | |
| 8. | Has destroyed school property, or that of other pupils. | | |
| 9. | Has physically abused other pupils/teacher/teaching assistant. | | |
| 10. | Has abused other pupils/teacher/teaching assistant verbally. | | |
| 11. | Often makes unnecessary non-verbal noise in class. | | |
| 12. | Is persistently late for school/lessons. | | |
| 13. | Will refuse to do work/homework. | | |
| 14. | Refuses to leave the room when asked. | | |
| 15. | Frequently loses temper. | | |

Other observations you wish to make.

Date:

© How to support and teach children with special educational needs LDA

Permission to Photocopy

# Hearing impairment

## Checklist

Name:                                        Observer:

| | | Yes | No |
|-----|---|-----|-----|
| 1. | Needs to concentrate on the teacher's mouth to understand language. | | |
| 2. | Shows unusually high level of frustration. | | |
| 3. | Displays an inability to understand what the teacher is saying. | | |
| 4. | Fails to understand verbal instructions. | | |
| 5. | Demonstrates tonal changes in speech. | | |
| 6. | Fails to respond to verbal cues. | | |
| 7. | Experiences persistent discharge from the ears. | | |
| 8. | Tilts head to maximise aural input. | | |
| 9. | Shows an increased reliance on peers for understanding or responding to instructions. | | |
| 10. | Exhibits emotional or behavioural problems not previously observed. | | |

Other observations you wish to make.

Date:

© How to support and teach children with special educational needs LDA                    Permission to Photocopy

# Visual impairment

## Checklist

Name:                                        Observer:

| | | Yes | No |
|---|---|---|---|
| 1. | Reading may be slow or hesitant. | | |
| 2. | Often becomes irritable or inattentive through frustration. | | |
| 3. | Squints or closes one eye when reading. | | |
| 4. | Narrows eyes and blinks a lot. | | |
| 5. | Often rubs eyes. | | |
| 6. | Moves/shades the book when reading. | | |
| 7. | Often loses place or omits lines or words when reading. | | |
| 8. | Has problems with columns or numbers. | | |
| 9. | Works too close to books for long periods. | | |
| 10. | Has a rigid body posture when viewing a distant object. | | |
| 11. | Complains frequently of headaches or eyestrain. | | |
| 12. | Finds copying from the board difficult. | | |
| 13. | Has difficulty trying to scan a page/follow a worksheet that contains a lot of writing. | | |
| 14. | Shows anxiety about certain physical activities or about being in the playground. | | |

Other observations you wish to make.

Date:

# References

## References

Cowne, Elizabeth (1998), *The SENCo Handbook: Working within a whole school approach*. London: David Fulton

Lee, Barbara (2002), *Teaching Assistants in Schools: The current state of play*. Windsor: NFER

Smith, Alistair (1996), *Accelerated Learning in the Classroom*. Stafford: Network Educational Press

Vass, Andy (2002), 'Ain't Misbehaving', *Times Educational Supplement*, December 6th edition

## Other sources

### Official documents
Education Act 1944

Central Advisory Council for Education (England) (1967) *Children and their Primary Schools* (The Plowden Report). London: HMSO

Handicapped Children's Act 1970

Department of Education and Science (1978) *Special Educational Needs* (The Warnock Report), HMSO

Education Act 1981

Department of Education and Science (1983–6) *The In-service Teacher Training Grants Scheme* (circulars 3/83, 4/84, 3/85), HMSO

Department for Education and Employment (1994a), *Code of Practice: on the Identification and Assessment of Special Educational Needs*, HMSO

Department for Education and Employment (1994b), *Education of Children with Emotional and Behavioural Difficulties* (circular 9/94), HMSO

Department for Education and Employment (1996), *Supporting Pupils with Medical Needs in School* (circular 14/96), HMSO

Department for Education and Employment/Department of Health (1996), *Supporting Pupils with Medical Needs. A good practice guide*, HMSO

Department for Education and Employment (1997), *Excellence for all Children: Meeting special educational needs*, HMSO

Special Educational Needs and Disability Act 2001 (SENDA)

Department for Education and Skills (2001), *Special Educational Needs Code of Practice* (581/2001)

Department for Education and Skills (2002), *Teaching Assistant File*, HMSO

# References continued

## Information sources

British Educational and Technology Communication Agency (BECTA)
*www.schools.becta.org.uk/inclusion*

Contact a Family (CAF)
*www.cafamily.org.uk*

## Practical resources

*Breaking the Code* (phonics tapes)
Learning Materials Limited

*Fuzz Buzz*
Oxford University Press

*PAT* (Phonological Awareness Training Scheme)
Educational Supply Publishers

*Wellington Square*
Nelson Thornes

*Single Sentences*
Easylearn

In addition, there are many excellent resources available for pupils with SEN. The following suppliers are particularly good.

Easylearn
Trent House
Fiskerton
Southwell
Nottinghamshire
NG25 OUH

LDA
Abbeygate House
East Road
Cambridge
CB1 1DB

Learning Materials Limited
Dixon Street
Wolverhampton
WV2 2BX

© *How to support and teach children with special educational needs* LDA

Permission to Photocopy